GURDJIEFF IN THE LIGHT OF TRADITION

A Treasury of Traditional Wisdom

*The Widening Breach: Evolutionism
in the Mirror of Cosmology*

Challenges to a Secular Society

The Unanimous Tradition (contributor)

WHITALL PERRY

GURDJIEFF
IN THE LIGHT
OF TRADITION

SOPHIA PERENNIS

GHENT NY

Second edition 2001
First edition, Perennial Books 1978
Originally published as a series of articles in
Studies in Comparative Religion 1974–75

For information, address:
Sophia Perennis, 343 Rte 21c
Ghent NY 12075

Library of Congress Cataloging-in-Publication Data

Perry, Whitall N.
Gurdjieff, in the light of tradition / Whitall N. Perry.

p. cm.
Originally published: Bedfont : Perennial Books, 1978.
Includes bibliographical references and index.
ISBN 0 900588 75 6 (pbk: alk. paper)
1. Gurdjieff, Georgi Ivanovitch, 1872–1949 I. Title.
B 4249.G84 13 P 38 2001
197—dc21   2001001185

CONTENTS

INTRODUCTION

This fellow doth not cast out devils, but by Beelzebub.
Matt. 12:26

*Understood from all sides not only different deep-rooted
minutia of the common psyche of man, suspected by me
and intriguing me all my life, but constated unexpectedly
many such 'delicacies', which had they been known to Mr
Beelzebub, would, I dare say, grow the horns mentioned by
me . . . even on his hooves.*
Gurdjieff

*If I had bared myself, I should inevitably have betrayed my
tail which there on your planet I skillfully hid under the
folds of my dress.*
Beelzebub, chap. 34

WHY Gurdjieff? Because despite René Guénon's warning
to 'flee Gurdjieff like the plague,' and although the man died before
the half-century mark reportedly saying to his intimates, '*Vous voilà
dans de beaux draps*' ('You're in a fine mess'), many people not
unfrequently endowed with real intellectual and spiritual potential
continue to follow his groups in France, England, Sweden, Germany, Switzerland, the United States, Australia, the Argentine, and
elsewhere, considering him as 'precursor of the New Age.' Three
errors almost invariably crop up when Gurdjieff's name is mentioned. First, that his work is acroamatic and cannot be properly
evaluated except by those on the 'inside': 'His science belongs to the
knowledge of antiquity,' writes Margaret Anderson, 'and this knowledge is transmitted by word of mouth, never written about except in
general terms.' This is nonsense, and her nephew, Fritz Peters,

rightly debunks what he calls the 'almost beatific secrecy' of this unknowability cult. Revelation, the source of all basic religions, is by nature *revelatory*, while the last thing esoterism in its limitless universality can mean is the exclusivism of *clique*; schools of philosophy likewise exist for the *dissemination* of ideas, whatever their relative merits, and to claim that there is an indefinable something — both ancient and yet new — which only an 'inner circle' of adepts can grasp is to subjectivize all possible approaches to understanding. Intelligence is by definition *intelligible*, and language — if words have sense — is the vehicle of communication. This observation is essential, since Gurdjieff/Ouspensky followers insist that the words can mean other than what they say, which if true would cast a grave responsibility on these authors for misleading countless readers. Tantra, Yoga, Hesychasm, Zen, Taoism, Vedānta, Platonism, Scholasticism, Hermeticism, the Kabbalah — let alone Freemasonry, occultism, secret societies, and pseudo-religions — ample documentation is there for all who care to find it; the only things 'hidden' are the particular techniques and formulas a master may give a disciple (although these are generally known *grosso modo*), and the extent of a person's inner comprehension and realization (though here again 'Ye shall know them by their fruits'). Naturally, if a thinker hoodwinks his thought in dark conundrums, riddles, mystification, and sundry obscure sophistries, then one is justified in brushing it off as just that. But when Peters goes on to say that 'the emotional experience that most people had with Gurdjieff and his work is not something that can be explained in a logical, convincing manner', this is altogether different, for here we are in the domain of pure subjectivity, and there is no question but what the personage under study had an emanation that was powerfully contagious to the individuals in his *entourage*.

The second error is one of perspective, that it is impossible to pierce through the aura of mystery and arrive at an objective assessment of the man since there are preponderantly two mutually exclusive views of equal validity each to the persons concerned: some claim to see a saint in him while others find a devil. *Au choix!* Somewhat as though there could be two schools of thought on whether London is nearer to Paris or Tokyo. Spiritual sciences on their level obey laws no less rigorous than physical sciences, and the criteria are there for those qualified to judge. This in no way means overlooking what we shall see to be Gurdjieff's enigmatic and contradictory character.

The third fallacy hinges on the idea that since Gurdjieff claimed to be the recipient of teachings transmitted from antiquity, all depends on being able to determine whether or not the spiritual organization(s) involved and the line(s) of transmission are authentic, valid, and orthodox; whereas the whole crux of the matter is contingent on whether he was himself a legitimate representative and faithful purveyor of any truths to which he may have been exposed. Mahesh Yogi, for example, stems from a spiritual lineage tracing back to Sankaracharya and is none the more orthodox for that, having perverted the practices of his order while pretending to be the first to reveal the heart of the Vedānta. It goes without saying that anyone purporting to come from the fastnesses of Central Asia with a teaching for the West about the regeneration of mankind could simplify matters enormously by presenting clear and unequivocal credentials. Gurdjieff, however, has a reply to this: if things were to be made too accessible it would draw unwanted elements into his path and obstruct the initiatic ends of his mission—a strange condition on the part of a 'scientific philosopher' (who practically considered himself an *avatāra*) with a 'manifesto' to humanity.

Documentation for this condensed study is drawn mainly from the following sources:

The Unknowable Gurdjieff, by Margaret Anderson (Routledge and Kegan Paul).

Our Life with Mr Gurdjieff, by Thomas de Hartmann (Penguin Books).

Gurdjieff Remembered, by Fritz Peters (Samuel Weiser).

In Search of the Miraculous, by P.D. Ouspensky (Routledge and Kegan Paul).

Witness: The Story of a Search, by John Godolphin Bennett (Coombe Springs Press).

Gurdjieff: Making a New World, J.G. Bennett (Turnstone Books).

Monsieur Gurdjieff, Louis Pauwels (Éditions du Seuil).
The Herald of Coming Good, G. Gurdjieff (Samuel Weiser).

It may be well to add that the seven works on Gurdjieff are far too unanimous in the portrait depicted to leave any doubt as to the intrinsic veracity and authenticity of the reporting; while the last book differs from the others only in that it reads like a caricature of this portrait.

Finally there is Gurdjieff's major opus: *Beelzebub's Tales to His Grandson. An Objectively Impartial Criticism of the Life of Man. All and Everything*, First Series (Routledge and Kegan Paul); and also the Second Series, *Meetings with Remarkable Men* and Third Series, *Life is Real Only Then, When 'I Am'* (Routledge and Kegan Paul).

1

THE BACKGROUND

GEORGE IVANOVITCH GURDJIEFF was born according to his passport on the 28th of December, 1877 (although he claimed to be much older), at Aleksandropol (formerly Gumru and now Leninakan) in northwest Armenia, of a Greek family originally named Georgiades from a peculiar culture anciently established in Asia Minor. He says his aged father—for whom he had a remarkable veneration and whose maxims he enjoyed repeating, such as 'If you wish to lose your faith, make friends with the priest'—was originally a wealthy cattle owner who lost his (and others') herds in a plague and had to turn to carpentry. This man was gifted as a local 'bard' or *ashokh* (he apparently knew the Gilgamesh epic) and *raconteur*; and certainly Gurdjieff inherited in no small degree the concomitant capacity for invention, which could explain in part, at least, his notoriety as a spinner of contradictory stories. On this point, moreover, his protagonists admit of no inconsistency, construing the trait as an allegorical lever for didactic purposes, while serving also as a consciously applied 'shock' technique or 'trial' to render the 'physical, emotional, and mental' substance of his disciples more resilient and aware. The truth probably falls somewhere between, Gurdjieff exploiting an idiosyncrasy of character as a tool for 'rectifying' the characters of others. Whatever the case, since the clues to his early training—apart from a few official documents and passports—lie solely in what he saw fit to divulge in his allegorical or what he calls 'legominnistic' manner, those determined to identify the sources of his message will have in large extent to decode the lineal tree(s) of his 'investiture' by the fruits which were to drop in later years.

This does not mean, however, that all must be left to conjecture: Gurdjieff was by his lights a logical—hence 'practical'—man, and much too 'real' a personality to countenance total duplicity. Already in his childhood he was fascinated by magical phenomena of diverse kinds, including religious miracles, and he realized forces were at play that could not be explained by the known laws of physics and biology. By the age of eleven, at which time he says he started drinking, having all his life an 'irresistible urge to do things not as others do them', he was frequenting the Romanys and Yezidis; when finally we find him organizing his own 'circle' in Tashkent around 1911, he had behind him a private training by the dean of the Kars Military Cathedral, for both priesthood and medicine—and some twenty years of prodigious peregrinations throughout Turkestan and the surrounding regions in pursuit of occult wisdom. Alone or with other 'Seekers of the Truth' he had penetrated more particularly Afghanistan, Kafiristan, Chitral, Kashmir, Sinkiang, Siberia, and Tibet or lands adjacent. He was brought up as much on Turkish as Armenian, which gave him a *lingua franca* for many of the places visited. He had likewise combed through Turkey, gone to what he claims was an Essene Jewish monastery near Jerusalem where he would have learned ritual dances based on a cycle of seven, studied Hesychasm at Mount Athos, and explored archaeological sites in Crete, Egypt, Abyssinia, and especially in the ruins of Babylon searching for traces of the 'Sarmân Brotherhood'—'Assembly of the Enlightened'—or 'Inner Circle of Humanity' said in an Armenian book *Merkhavat* to have been founded there some four thousand four hundred years ago. The word Sarmân or Sarmoun appears in certain Pahlavi texts to designate the custodians of Zoroaster's teaching. He learned more about Zoroastrianism from his contacts with the Yezidis of Kurdistan at Sheikh Adi and Mosul, who in addition would have divulged their traditions inherited from Mithraism and Manichaeism.

❂

Gurdjieff writes that he had 'the possibility of gaining access to the so-called 'holy-of-holies' of nearly all hermetic organizations such as religious, philosophical, occult, political and mystic societies, congregations, parties, unions, etc., which were inaccessible to the ordinary man, and of discussing and exchanging views with innumerable people who, in comparison with others, are real authorities.' He even professes to have made the Pilgrimage to Mecca and Medina with Sart Dervishes, although nothing came of it, as orthodox Islam held little attraction for him. He believed, however, that northern Sufi orders could well be under the hidden direction of the Khwajagân—'Masters of Wisdom'—themselves in turn delegated by the Sarmân 'Inner Circle', the 'Assembly-of-All-the-Living-Saints-of-the-Earth'. We know how people were haunted at that period with the idea of a spiritual World Center concealed in the heart of Asia (Saint-Yves d'Alveydre with his 'Agarttha' and Madame Blavatsky with her 'Shambala')[1] from which an 'Elite' directs the destiny of humanity somewhat in the way that people earlier were intrigued right into the Renaissance with the idea that the Terrestrial Paradise might possibly still exist in some unattainable region on earth. Anyhow, Bokhara and not Mecca was for him the secret center of Islam, where the Naqshbandîya Sufis—supposedly infiltrated by the Khwajagân—were concentrated until the close of the nineteenth century; and it is from them that J. G. Bennett thinks Gurdjieff adopted many ideas and techniques. The programme for the 'movements' demonstrations which his group was to give in Paris and New York meanwhile attributes the sources of the 'dances' and 'rituals' to monasteries in Sari in Tibet, Mazari Sherif in Afghanistan, Kizilgan in the Keriya Oasis in Chinese Turkestan, and Yangi Hissar in Kashgar. Gurdjieff also writes that he had access in Central Asia 'into a monastery well known among the followers of the Mahometan religion' where he became 'absolutely convinced that the answers for which I was looking . . . can only be found . . . in the sphere of "man's subconscious mentation"'; again, that he went 'to a certain Dervish monastery, situated likewise in Central Asia,' where

---

1. Thanks to information supplied by a Hindu friend and scholar, we hear that these two Sanskrit terms have a venerable origin, appearing in an ancient Tibetan text, *The Road to Shambala*. This latter word designates 'Abode of Siva', while Agarttha means 'ungraspable'; and in the context Shambala represents a transcendent Center, Agarttha being the same Center hidden in the earth.

he spent two years in the study of hypnotism and 'the mechanism of the functioning of man's subconscious sphere.' Bennett guesses that this must have been a *tekki* (community center) of the Yesevi order, a fraternity founded by the shaman-raised Ahmed Yesevi (born about 1042)—the first of the Turkish Khwajas and called by the Turks Bab-Arslan, or Lion Father-at Yesi which was to become Tashkent. Because of their affiliations with shamanism the present-day Yesevis are said to be unfavorably regarded by other Sufi orders, but this affinity is just what would argue favorably with Gurdjieff, given their stress on cosmology, and the use of music, rhythm, magic, shock techniques, and perhaps also the 'stop exercise'[2] which was later to feature in his method. Another clue dropped by Gurdjieff refers to the religious exercises of the Matchna monks in the eastern Gobi desert who had connections both with the Yesevis and with Tibetan tantric Buddhism. All this is very complicated; but then, Gurdjieff was not a simple man.

❂

A word must be inserted here on the subject of shamanism. In his chapter 'Shamanism and Sorcery' in *The Reign of Quantity and the Signs of the Times*, Guénon explains that the religion practiced by various Mongol peoples is essentially *primordial*[3] in origin, with rites comparable to those of the Vedic tradition; in certain sectors, however, there has been an over-development of the cosmological sciences, leading to a preoccupation with the animic domain and the manipulation of powers belonging to the inferior psychic realm with the attendant accumulation of magical forces, which can present a real—if local—danger to the shaman himself, but is nothing compared to the generalized danger that accrues when these potent magical residues are captured by people with quite other ends in view than the shaman himself—a mere instrument

2. Discussed in the next section.
3. It is noteworthy that followers of Gurdjieff take pride in belonging to a 'primordial current' that 'transcends' the different religions.

for condensing these forces—could ever dream of. Whether or not in writing these passages Guénon had someone like Gurdjieff in sight, it is certain that Gurdjieff for all the doors he may or may not have been able to open did not leave these monasteries with his bags empty. He even told Bennett in later times about acquiring powers: 'If you wish to acquire something of your own, you must learn to steal.'

How, meanwhile, did he maintain himself throughout those years? By trading in antiques and carpets and corsets, for one thing, and manufacturing bric-a-brac, repairing broken machinery, and organizing various rural enterprises 'of a rather questionable character';[4] for another, by serving very probably as an agent for the Russian government. He says he was 'almost mortally . . . wounded three times in quite different circumstances' through being 'punctured' by a 'stray bullet'. The first time was in Crete in 1896 just before the outbreak of the Greco-Turkish War, where he may have arrived as a member of the Ethniki Etaireia, a subversive society supported by the Russian government to foment trouble in Macedonia. The second time was in Tibet in 1902 on the eve of the 'Anglo-Tibetan War'. Gurdjieff talked of his 'Tibetan marriage' and how his eldest son had been appointed the abbot of an important lamasery. He could well have been in Tibet as a Russian political

---

4. This 'cunning old blade'—as Gurdjieff described himself at that period—tells how he was resting in the shade of trees in New Samarkand devising schemes to finance his travels, when he observed a number of sparrows in the branches above. Knowing the fondness of the Sarts in this region for songbirds, he forthwith searched out the nearest cabstand, where the drivers were dozing in the afternoon heat, and surreptitiously plucked from the horses' tails the hairs needed to make snares for the sparrows.

With the first bird netted he repaired to his lodgings and clipped its feathers to the semblance of a canary, which he then colored fantastically with aniline dyes he had on hand for painting artificial paper flowers. This *rara avis* was peddled off in the markets of Old Samarkand for two roubles as a special 'American canary', the proceeds paying for several cheap painted cages, soon to lodge more luckless 'canaries'. By the end of a fortnight our habile huckster had made a small fortune with the sale of some eighty caged, clipped, and painted sparrows, whereupon he took the next train out of town before a sudden rain or an inadvertent bath in their drinking troughs should expose the birds'—and his—true colors.

agent, where his name would have been pronounced Doffieff since according to him there is no 'g' in Tibetan, but Bennett says the inference that he might have been the famous Lama Dorjieff who was a tutor of the Dalai Lama and later his emissary to Tsar Nicholas II crumbles before the photographic evidence.[5]

The third 'stray bullet' was 'plunked' into him in 1904 in the Trans-Caucasian region near Chiatur,

> by some 'milashka' from among those two groups of people . . . the so-called Russian Army, chiefly Cossacks, and the so-called Gourians.

These remarks heighten the hypothesis that he was both 'running with the hare and hunting with the hounds,' being caught up in the revolutionary movement, possibly in the same group with the Georgian Djugashivill, later to be known to the world as Joseph Stalin. It has recently been conjectured that Stalin at that time was playing the double role of Tsarist agent in the secret police (Okhrana) and revolutionary. Gurdjieff, of course, claims to have known Stalin and to have studied with him in the seminary at Aleksandropol. He grants his

> propensity during this period for . . . trying to place myself wherever . . . there proceeded sharp energetic events, such as civil wars, revolution, etc.,

always in view of gaining more information about man's hidden motivations, and to

---

5. An expert on Tibet states that in Tibetan G is a particularly common letter. Witness such words as *gon-pa*—monastery, *gang*—who? which? *ge-long*—*bhikku*—fully ordained monk, *gur-ma*—hymn (same initial syllable as Gurdjieff!); how could a person who had studied in Tibet be ignorant of such a fact? On the other hand, F is absent from the Tibetan alphabet; the final letter of Gurdjieff could not be reproduced exactly. (It is possible that if he said he had visited Tibet, he meant Ladak, sometimes known as 'Little Tibet', which, forming part of the state of Kashmir at that time, would have been relatively accessible; but even so, this does not explain his alleged statement that G is wanting in the language.) ED.

discover, at all costs, some manner or means for destroying in people the predilection for suggestibility which causes them to fall easily under the influence of 'mass-hypnosis'.

The solution he sought flashed upon him during a transformation of character that he would have undergone during convalescence in an eastern retreat from one of his bullet wounds, a transition leading to what Bennett calls 'liberation from the "pairs of opposites"' that Gurdjieff supposedly achieved in his thirty-second year. His autobiographical account of this insight is given in the *Third Series* of his writings, entitled *Life is Real Only Then, When 'I Am'*:[6]

> He had developed by this time highly concentrated psychic and hypnotic powers, and was frankly becoming something of a menace: people called him 'the Tiger of Turkestan'. For all his mental prowess, he was 'haunted by the terror of "inner emptiness"', and felt it urgent to attain a permanent awareness that would free him from the tyranny and conditioning of automatic hereditary factors to have outside myself, so to say, 'A never-sleeping-factor, a reminding-factor.' Namely, a factor which would remind me always, in my every common state, to 'remember myself'. But what is this!!! Can it be really so??! A new thought!!! Why could not I, in this instance also, look to a 'universal analogy'? And here also is God!!!...'
>
> God represents absolute goodness; He is all-loving and all-forgiving. He is the just Pacifier of all that exists. At the same time, why should He, being as He is, send away from Himself one of his nearest, by Him animated, Beloved Sons, only for the 'way of pride' proper to any young and still incompletely formed individual, and bestow upon Him a force equal but opposite to His own? . . . I refer to the 'Devil'. This idea illuminated the condition of my inner world like the sun, and rendered it obvious that in the great world for the possibility of harmonious construction there was inevitably required some kind of continuous perpetuation of the reminding factor. For this reason our Maker Himself, in the name of all that He had created, was compelled to place

6. The extracts which follow are given in Bennett's *New World*.

one of His Beloved Sons in such an, in the objective sense, invidious situation. Therefore I also have now for my small inner world to create out of myself, from some factor beloved by me an alike unending source. . . .
I came to the conclusion, that if I should intentionally stop utilizing the exceptional power in my possession which had been developed by me consciously in my common life with people, then there must be forced out of me such a reminding source. Namely, the power based upon strength in the field of *hanbledzoin* or as it would be called by others, power of telepathy and hypnotism. . . . And so, if consciously I would deprive myself of this grace of my inherence, then undoubtedly always and in everything its absence would be felt. Never as long as I live shall I forget what state of mind resulted then.

Translated, this means that Gurdjieff resolved to forego the role of thaumaturge for his own aggrandizement and glory, and to transmit instead to those whom he considered qualified, his high-energy *hanbledzoin* as a 'reminding-factor' for the good of mankind, in view of ultimately awakening humanity from its 'mass-hypnosis'; and to judge from the state of things, it appears that a good deal of this force remains in circulation these many years after his death. Bennett writes that

Gurdjieff was, more than anything else, a Sufi. . . . The true way transmits a spiritual power, *baraka* or *hanbledzoin*, which enables the seeker to do what is quite beyond his unaided strength. . . . This transmission of a higher energy that can be assimilated to the energy of the pupil is a vital part of the whole process, and in this sense it certainly can be said that Gurdjieff, at all times, was a teacher. Everyone who met him reported the sense of mastery, of a power which acted upon them. . . . Sometimes, when the people could not perform the difficult tasks which he set them, he would tell them to 'draw on my *hanbledzoin* and you will be able to do this work'. . . . He also, though not so specifically, referred to himself as being in contact with a higher source, and said that by drawing upon this higher source, the work for which he was responsible would be able to spread and gain strength in the world. . . . I think he wished to convey to us that we should, after his death . . . become a means for the transmission of this higher energy.

The reader will not fail to notice in the long citation from Gurdjieff above, his divergence with Christian theology as to the identity of the Beloved Son sent into the world to redeem mankind; for him, in fact, the 'Logos' without the participation of a 'Neutralizing third force' (*fagologiria*) is purely 'sterile'.

Gurdjieff, incidentally, called psychoanalysis 'nonsense', but there is notwithstanding an inescapable similarity in the remedial techniques developed by him and Sigmund Freud: both men made the 'contribution' of turning magic into a therapeutic device; what Freud calls 'the inhibitions of instinct' that have to be eradicated corresponds with what Gurdjieff calls 'the influence of "mass-hypnosis"'; the transference operated by the psychoanalyst through 'playing the Devil' or acting as a 'counterwill' (the 'suspended superego') to his patient's will in order to cure the 'neurosis'[7] corresponds with Gurdjieff's transmission of *hanbledzoin* as a 'reminding factor' or 'counterhypnosis' in order to cure man of the 'psychosis' of his propensity to suggestibility, namely, 'the automatic manifestations of his nature'—the Devil[8] (reminding source) being 'forced out' to exorcize the 'demon' (hereditary factors)—'mercilessly, without any compromise whatsoever, to extirpate from the mentation and feeling of man the previous, century-rooted views and beliefs about everything existing in the world.'[9]

7. An intensive study on Freudianism, its background and ramifications, is given in 'The Revolt Against Moses: A New Look at Psychoanalysis', by Whitall N. Perry, published in the Spring 1966 number of *Tomorrow*.

8. Peters writes that Gurdjieff 'called himself a "devil".' Freud likewise said: 'Do you not know that I am the Devil? All my life I have had to play the Devil, in order that others would be able to build the most beautiful cathedral with the materials that I produced' (R. Laforgue, 'Persönliche Erinnerungen an Freud', *Lindauer Psychotherapiewoche*, 1954, p 49).

9. From the preamble to *All and Everything*, as given in *The Herald of Coming Good*, p 47.

❂

Back to Tashkent: it is in this Uzbekian oasis of Eastern and Western cultures, where shamanism, Buddhism, and Islam were practiced alongside Nestorian and Russian Orthodox Christianity—with a sprinkling of occult and theosophical societies on the fringe—that Gurdjieff first set himself up around 1910 as a mage, professional hypnotist, healer, and wonderworker. He frequented the divers occultist organizations, which served for him as ready-to-hand 'workshops-for-the-perfection-of-psychopathism' where he could 'observe and study various manifestations in the waking state of the psyche of these trained and freely moving "Guinea-Pigs", allotted to me by Destiny for my experiments.' Results were rapid, and within six months he was becoming well known as an 'expert' and 'a great "maestro"'. But his 'workshops' proved too narrow in scope, affording him no more than three or four human types out of the needed '28 "categories-of-types" existing on Earth, as they were established in ancient times.' He thus founded his 'own "circle" on quite new principles, with a staff of people chosen specially by me,' and from which was later to emerge the Institute for the Harmonious Development of Man. His efforts to introduce the hidden teachings of the 'Masters of Wisdom' to mankind at large were claimed to have been sanctioned through 'a certain definite agreement' that he secured from a 'brotherhood' or 'kind of monastery existing in the very heart of Asia' for 'their future co-operation'; by different clues that were dropped, Bennett takes this to be a Sarmân sanctuary in the Keriya Oasis (Sinkiang) that presumably proffered guidance for the remainder of Gurdjieff's career.

Apart from the money he 'sheared from disciples,' Gurdjieff tells how he kept himself in funds at this time, by arranging contracts for road and railway construction; buying and selling stores, restaurants, and cinemas; driving cattle; participating in oil wells and fisheries; and dealing in rugs, Chinese porcelain, and cloisonné. Then in emergencies he could always fall back on his healing powers: 'There was not a single book on neuropathology and psychology in the library of Kars Military Hospital that I had not read and read very attentively.' Bennett saw him 'cure drug addicts and drunkards' in Turkey in 1921, and says that he repeated this later in Paris to help finance construction on the Prieuré at Avon near Fontainebleau, the final home of the Institute. And Peters tells how he witnessed the same thing in New York around 1935, when Gurdjieff was without other resources:

> I became acquainted with a stream of 'patients'—at least they were not the usual 'followers'—who came to him regularly for 'treatments' of various kinds. Most of them were afflicted with something: they were alcoholics, dope-addicts, just plain neurotics, homosexuals, and what could be called 'adult delinquents' of one kind or another. I gathered that they paid him well to 'cure' them of whatever disease or manifestation happened to be afflicting them. I do not know in what the cures consisted,[10] except that all of them required long and frequent visits with him at all hours of the day or night.... The effect on the individuals was the usual one: they worshipped him, at least temporarily....
> This period of having to earn money did not last very long, and it was a relief to me when it was over [and] he emerged from this rather woebegone characterization of a kind of quack-doctor living in shoddy circumstances.... The derelicts also vanished from the scene.

In 1911 Gurdjieff took a 'special oath' binding himself in conscience to lead for the next twenty-one years 'in some ways an artificial ... and, for me, absolutely unnatural life.' This may have helped in the accumulation of *hanbledzoin*; it certainly helped give a rationale to his eccentric and somewhat licentious behavior which was to confuse his disciples when he came to Moscow and St Petersburg in 1912 in search of a wider range of personality-types for his expanding 'workshop'. Thus, when Gurdjieff's illustrious disciple, Peter Demianovitch Ouspensky, first met his master in Moscow in 1915, he was

---

10. In *Meetings with Remarkable Men*, Gurdjieff says it was through hypnotism: 'After bringing a man into a certain state, [I] could influence him by suggestion to forget any undesirable habit.'

discomfited by

> the strange, unexpected, and almost alarming impression of a man poorly disguised, the sight of whom embarrasses you because you see he is not what he pretends to be and yet you have to speak and behave as though you did not see it. . . . Many people got the impression that he was a gourmand, a man fond of good living in general, and it seemed to us that he often *wanted* to create this impression, although all of us already saw that this was 'acting'. . . . In any other man so much 'acting' would have produced an impression of falsity. In him 'acting' produced an impression of strength, although . . . not always; sometimes there was too much of it.

And Thomas de Hartmann, who at that time was a reserve Guards officer, writes: 'I must say that my first reaction was anything but one of rapture or veneration.' He was constrained to meet Gurdjieff in a cafe of such character that

> if anyone were to find out that I had been there, I would have had to leave my regiment. . . . At one point Mr Gurdjieff said, 'There are usually more whores here.' Everything, including this coarse observation, was supposed not to attract but rather to repel a newcomer. Or if not to repel him, at least to make him hurdle the difficulties, holding fast to his aim in spite of everything.

It is not at all uncommon, as is well known, for spiritual masters to test the mettle of potential disciples through rude ordeals of one kind or another, but there are limits and degrees and modalities-even so.

Gurdjieff, inevitably, found his way into the ill-starred court of Nicholas (whose person he respected, if not his polity) and Alexandra, from whose entourage he took to wife a lady-in-waiting, the Polish-born Countess Ostrowska. He was not the first wonder-worker to arrive, having been preceded by such 'luminaries'—given entrance through the spiritualist *salon noir* of the Countess Ignatiev—as Maître Philippe, the former butcher's boy from Lyon become hypnotist and healer, and named through the Tsarina's insistence 'Russian military doctor' (not recognized by France) with the rank of army general and membership in the Council of State presided over by the Tsar, and who before he was expulsed foretold the immanent coming to the Romanoffs of a 'messenger of God'; Papus (Dr Gérard Encausse), the celebrated magnetizer, occultist, Martinist-Freemason, and disciple of Philippe, who—the same as Rasputin—correctly predicted that his own death would coincide with the outbreak of the Revolution; Mitia Kobita, the one-armed hunchback and 'fool in Jesus Christ', a stutterer only able to pronounce 'Papa' and 'Mama' and yet considered an 'oracle', who in one or another fashion served as a secret counsellor to the Tsar; the sorceress Dania Ossipova who counselled Nicholas II on the war with Japan; the magician and illuminé Antoni, who was likewise a political counsellor; and then again, the strange thaumaturge Dr Yamsarane Badmaliev (called 'the owl' and 'the bug') who was initiated in his native Mongolia to Tibetan medicine and magic, and was later to attend the University at St. Petersburg for a polishing in politics and diplomacy—Tsar Alexander III consented to be the godfather of this personage who, while directing a laboratory and clinic for healing neurotics with 'Tibetan elixirs', was destined to become the most powerful of all secret counsellors to Nicholas II: no high post was filled by the Tsar except upon his recommendation. The stage was thus thoroughly set for the grand entrance of Rasputin, who would soon far eclipse all these minor precursors—excepting, of course, Gurdjieff, said to be canvassed by the moderates in the court as a foil to the dreaded machinations of the mesmeric monk. Too late, however; the die was cast.

❂

Rasputin's assassination and the death of Papus both happened in 1916, and as predicted, all hell broke loose. It broke loose in the soul of poor de Hartmann also, who gives a graphic and excruciating account of the trials endured by Gurdjieff and his loyal band of followers to maintain the 'Institute for the Harmonious Development of Man' amidst the crossfire of the Cossacks and the Bolsheviks. Nor was 'Mr Gurdjieff'—as de Hartmann always refers to him—

ever one to pass up an occasion for 'entangling' (his expression) things even further. Thus one evening in Essentuki in the Caucasus where they took refuge in 1917, at a time when the rouble was disastrously devalued, Gurdjieff manoeuvred the impoverished de Hartmann—cut off from his monthly funds—into hosting a banquet at a restaurant, where five-hundred roubles were needed to cover a meal that formerly cost two to three, and the bill came to about one thousand; a waiter had to be tipped to rouse a frightened Mme de Hartmann from bed, who surrendered what amounted to half a month's living expenses. Gurdjieff reimbursed his victim the next morning, while simply saying, 'What happened was done for your sake.' On another occasion, the hapless composer was first obliged to sacrifice precious music paper reserved for the orchestration of a ballet, by stripping it into reels for winding skeins of silk, and then was ignominiously sent to sell the silk to his former acquaintances from St Petersburg now living in Kislovodsk. He naturally enough avoided his friends, slipping at dusk into a large shop owned by his landlord—where he found Gurdjieff awaiting him. The silk was disposed of, and they returned home. De Hartmann saw this as a 'wonderful lesson' in surmounting the 'sense of class pride'. His wife was also given a lesson in 'selflessness' when forced to hand over all her family jewels to Gurdjieff—who then replied, 'Now take them back.' Inspired by this magnanimity, another lady offered up her valuables. That was the last she saw of them. 'Everything that could repel, even frighten', in de Hartmann's words, was integral to his master's methods.

Civil war soon rendered life in Essentuki intolerable, and Gurdjieff devised a scheme for escaping into the Caucasus mountains by proposing to organize an archaeological expedition in search of dolmens while at the same time planting a rumor that he knew of vast deposits of gold and platinum in the same region that could bring enormous wealth to the Provincial Government: people, as he wished to demonstrate to his pupils, will 'believe any old tale.' The Essentuki Soviet forwarded the request to the higher Soviet in Piatigorsk, who offered unlimited facilities, including two railway wagons to take the party to Maikop in 1918 when rail travel was almost exclusively reserved for troop movements. Ouspensky, who did not accompany the expedition, said that a large amount of alcohol would be needed for 'washing the gold'. Gurdjieff got the message, and the government came through with gallons of pure spirits—otherwise unobtainable—which were divided among the party in bottles labelled 'Medicine for the treatment of cholera,' while another portion that was denatured was rendered potable by filtering through hot bread and baked onions and then put into bottles marked 'Medicine for the treatment of malaria.'

Gurdjieff was able to get the necessary papers and new Soviet passports for the group of some thirty persons; he trained the men and women to carry seventy and fifty-pound packs respectively by practicing with stone-weighted rucksacks; he taught them navigation by the stars and how to walk in mountains at night. 'The rules were Draconian,' writes de Hartmann:

> we were no longer to be husbands or wives, or brothers, or sisters, to one another: we had to accept for the duration of the expedition unquestioning obedience to the leader, Mr Gurdjieff. As the expedition would involve us in deadly perils, we had to fulfill every order exactly; disobedience would be punishable even by death, and saying this Mr Gurdjieff put a large revolver on the table.

From Maikop they journeyed south eastward with pack animals over the mountains, criss-crossing the Bolshevik and White Army lines at least five times, and having little but faith in their leader's experienced resourcefulness to hold them together through every conceivable difficulty—including a foray with highwaymen—until finally they reached the Black Sea town of Sochi. The day before, in the hills above, they had triumphantly discovered a dolmen—though no gold—with the help of some hunters who were dumbfounded when Gurdjieff took measurements and revealed still two more that were completely unknown to these men of the region.

Then in January, 1919, they continued to Tiflis, the capital of Georgia, where the old regime yet existed. The Municipal Council lent a hand in getting the Institute re-established, and it was here in this community still flourishing with cultural life that the painter Alexander de Salzmann and his wife Jeanne, who was then teaching the Dalcroze system of dancing, joined the group, where their expertise was exploited for the choreography.

We next find the group—now reshuffled—in Turkey on its way to Europe, in June 1920—a country easier of entry than exit for Gurdjieff, since the authorities had received a dispatch from New Delhi warning that he was a 'very dangerous Russian agent,' with the result that he was considered suspect and thus unable to obtain permission to leave the land. Not one to sit on his hands, Gurdjieff responded by opening a branch of the Institute in Constantinople, where he went hard to work on his master ballet, 'The Struggle of the Magicians', and had his troupe stage among other things supernatural phenomena such as hypnotism, action at a distance, and thought transference.

In 1921 Gurdjieff was able to move on to Germany, where he thought of taking over the idled Dalcroze Institute of Eurythmic Dance at Hellerau near Dresden; but an invitation from Lady Rothermere and other rich friends of Ouspensky who was now in London tempted him to come to England, and there might he have stayed had not the Home Office refused him and his group visas extending beyond one month.

❈

The following phase of this indefatigable career opens at Avon near Fontainebleau, forty miles from Paris, in the summer of 1922, where Mme de Hartmann in the role of secretary to Gurdjieff came upon an abandoned mansion with weed-infested park, that had been remodelled from a seventeenth-century monastery for Priors and now called the Chateau du Prieuré, said to have once been the residence of Madame de Maintenon. It was presently the property of the widow of Maître Labori, the famous lawyer who defended Dreyfus and who received as recompense from the Dreyfus family this estate. The asking price was a million francs, and although Gurdjieff had exhausted his funds in getting his pupils moved from Germany to France, he gave out the order from Paris to have the place purchased, sight unseen. Olga de Hartmann practiced on the widow the persuasion techniques learned from her Master and was able to secure some sort of lease with the option to buy. A call for help was then launched to the wealthy, while Gurdjieff with his usual acumen opened a clinic in Paris for drunkards and dope addicts, ventured in Azerbaijan oil, and aided Russian émigrés in starting restaurants in Montmartre which later paid off handsome dividends. All this, moreover, with the initial need for interpreters, thus rendering more difficult of achievement that instant psychic grip which he counted on establishing with clients.

By November the Prieuré was aswarm with disciples and visitors of many nationalities and callings, both rich and poor, artists, writers, doctors, professors, and musicians, from bejewelled American widows to ragged poets, all of whom except the transients and decrepit were put to Herculean tasks from dawn to sundown, building, felling trees, sawing timber, caring for a multitude of domestic animals, toiling in the kitchen, house, and laundry, tending the flower and vegetable gardens, and then at day's end, changing for dinner, followed by an evening of 'Sacred Gymnastics', or perhaps a lecture by Gurdjieff, or some old tunes on his little accordion-piano. Around midnight he would disdainfully call out: '*Kto hochet spat, mojet itti spat*,' or 'Who want sleep go sleep'; but few would leave, knowing that the real teachings were reserved only for those who persevered to the breaking-point of endurance.

The grounds featured a 'Study House' constructed from a surplus Zeppelin hangar obtained from the French Air Force for the cost of removal; it was before long converted into a kind of pseudo-Oriental pavilion replete with priceless Asian rugs, hangings, cushions, goatskins, raised divans, visitors' benches, a stage with the Enneagram[11] figured above and a special box or 'Kosshah' for 'Mr Gurdjieff', fountains with fish (or on exceptional occasion champagne), colored lights, and of course—a grand piano. All pupils had to remove their shoes before entering, and the men were grouped separately from the women. For de Hartmann it created 'the impression of a mosque,' although in place of Qur'ânic inscriptions, the cloth ceiling featured aphorisms by Gurdjieff painted and

---

11. Explained in the next section.

embroidered in a special script of his invention which read verti-
cally and suggested a jumble of Oriental alphabets disincarnate as a
dream. The disciples were required to learn this lettering and ponder such arcane platitudes as:

> I love him who loves work; The best means of obtaining felicity
> in this life is the ability to consider externally always, internally
> never [sic]; Take the understanding of the East and the knowl-
> edge of the West, and then seek; The highest achievement of man
> is to be able TO DO; [and so forth].

Gurdjieff—or 'G' as his intimates referred to him—christened his
quarters on the second floor of the Prieuré The Ritz, where he set up
in the manner of a pasha. Photographs taken at this period portray
a stocky Levantine character with dome-like shaven head, huge
baleful eyes, and a fierce moustache tucked between cheeks that
hide a sarcastic glimmer of the mischievous and comic.

He drove his charges like a Turk to wake them out of their inherited stain of 'complacency', sauntering through the grounds tar-
boosh aslant and puffing at long black cigarettes (although smoking
was discountenanced for the others less advanced in their Harmonious Development), cajoling, praising, and cursing by turns. His
rages, however simulated, were terrible to behold, for 'his entire
body would shake, his face grow purple and a stream of vitupera-
tion would pour out,' to cite Bennett. But he was also capable of dis-
pensing sweets—both literally and figuratively; and yet if a disciple
mastered a chore or betrayed pleasure in his task, he risked being
promptly reassigned to something disagreeable. No one dared complain; even the flies infesting the kitchen were tolerated as a 'test'.
Without Gurdjieff's organizational skill and mastery of every art
and craft from musical arrangement and Eastern cooking, to animal
husbandry, masonry, stonecraft, agronomy, tailoring, carpentry,
and the repair of electrical equipment, the place would have come
apart at the seams; and yet precisely because of his Asiatic miscom-
prehension of Europeans' capacity for effort, there were those who
cracked physically, emotionally, and psychically, with more than
one death and suicide. Peters absolves him of responsibility for
Katherine Mansfield's death, however, arguing justifiably that she

was already wasted with tuberculosis when she arrived at Fontainebleau, and that it was her affair if she chose to shorten her days there rather than prolonging them in a sanatorium. Still, it seems rather excessive having this frail creature quartered in the stable over the cows in the damp cold of winter, purportedly to benefit from the bovine exhalations—physical and 'spiritual'.

Life at the Prieuré was not entirely Spartan; there were diversions, such as the motorcade-picnics, a joy to all but those who had to be in his huge open landau when Gurdjieff instead of the Russian chauffeur took the wheel. Provided plans did not change at the last moment, and provided the cars could make the steep uphill run leading into the forests of Fontainebleau, and provided one of the frequent mechanical failures did not materialize, the cortege of his 'calves' cruised into the country, hampers charged like cornucopias with caviar and melons, and awash with champagne, armagnac, and vodka. Then a halt might be called in some tumble-down village, the party trooping into a cafe, where Gurdjieff flourishing a wallet stuffed with thousand-franc notes would order drinks for all present, and maybe treat the local citizenry with an air on the single-handed accordion, or, on later excursions, write a few snatches of *Beelzebub* at a sidewalk table.

And Peters remembers his joy as a child at Fontainebleau the day Gurdjieff on a whim bought two hundred bicycles and ordered everyone out riding them. But the biggest occasions were the Saturday feast days, when 'the Forest Philosophers'—as the devotees were called—gave public evening demonstrations of their dances and staged pseudo-magical phenomena. These evenings also featured a special banquet dedicated to the 'Science of Idiotism', said to be derived from an ancient Central Asian institution called the *Chamodar*, or Master of the Feast. Gurdjieff had learned from a 'Sufi community' that there are twenty-one gradations of reason or 'idiotism' in man's evolution from his natural 'reasonless' state to the highest state of 'Our Endlessness', or 'God'. As the last three states are reserved for God and his sons, that left open within the generic category of 'All Hopeless Idiots' eighteen specific grades to choose from, each person being free to decide what type of idiotism best accorded with his nature,—the compassionate idiot, the squirming idiot, the zigzag, doubting, swaggering, or enlightened idiot, as the case might be. The 'ancient sages' taught that alcohol was used to actualize one's degree of idiotism. Dr Christopher Evans has amusingly if not very flatteringly described this event in his *Cults of Unreason*:

> At these sessions Gurdjieff who was a great tippler, would call a long series of toasts to various kinds of 'idiot', in which all, whether teetotallers or not, were obliged to participate. It was a great evening for those who liked alcohol, and a nightmare for those who didn't. The Russian's many biographers, great and small, have made numerous attempts at explaining the significance of the 'idiots' toast', and most have come to the conclusion that the not particularly ambiguous word had some symbolic significance. No one, it seems, has ever seriously contemplated the possibility that the idiots in question were those seated at the table, though one suspects that Gurdjieff with fez awry and flushed, beaming face, had a pretty good idea of whom he was thinking as he raised his glass on high.

❂

By December 1923, the dances and music were perfected to the point that a performance was able to be given at the Théâtre des Champs Elysées. This in turn led to an invitation for the Master impresario and his troupe to demonstrate their theatrics in America. Here again Gurdjieff showed his organizational skill, arranging for complete outfits of clothing, and getting passports validated for the Russians, Lithuanians, Armenians, and Poles in the group. Early in 1924 they sailed to New York on the 'Paris', 'Mr Gurdjieff' occupying a first-class cabin, the others berthed in second; the company was allowed the use of the first-class lounges, however, in exchange for a performance of the 'movements' on behalf of the crew. The crossing was particularly rough, and de Hartmann recalls the night of the spectacle with Gurdjieff in the front row suddenly shouting, 'Stop!' and the dancers in frozen contortions slithering to starboard, then to port, while 'the piano slowly, but steadily, slid from one side of the stage to the other, myself following it on my chair.'

With the help of rich admirers, concert halls were hired in New York, where Walter Damrosch himself attended a performance, in Philadelphia and Boston, where they played to Harvard University professors and students, then Chicago, with finally a gala demonstration given at Carnegie Hall in April before the company returned to France to prepare a second American tour for the following autumn.

These plans were shattered by an automobile accident in July that almost cost Gurdjieff his life, and brought the Institute to a jarring halt. In his words:

> As a final chord, this battered physical body of mine crashed with an automobile going at a speed of ninety kilometers an hour into a very thick tree...alongside the road in Fontainebleau forest...one week [it was actually several] after my return to Europe from America. From such a 'promenade', it was discovered that I was not destroyed and several months later, to my misfortune, into my totally mutilated body there returned in full force, with all its former attributes, my consciousness.

He must have had a premonition of this accident, for it was imputed to a faulty steering wheel on his Citroen, which he had just had checked at a garage before taking the calamitous drive. He anyhow saw the mishap as 'the manifestation of a power hostile to his aim, a power with which he could not contend'—in Bennett's words.

Gurdjieff was transported almost immediately from the hospital at Avon to the Prieuré, where he regained consciousness after five days, but recovery came very slowly. De Hartmann writes that as soon as he

> was able to get up and stroll about with the help of his wife or one of us, he began to ask to have tall trees cut down to make big bonfires in the park almost every day.... Fire evidently pleased Mr Gurdjieff; we thought that he drew a kind of force from it, and we tried to provide him with as many as possible. But the felling of the trees was a difficult matter.

Did it not occur to de Hartmann that there might also have been an element of vengeance here against 'a very thick tree'?

This was a bad time for the founder of the now paralyzed Institute. His mother was dying, his wife was dying, the Russians—helpless refugees in a land where few knew the language and their one idol lay stricken—sat huddled, crushed, in the corridors of the chateau; virtually all of the English departed, 'with their tails between their legs'—in Gurdjieff's idiom, and about the only financial support remaining for the heavily indebted Institute was from the journalist and critic, Alfred Richard Orage, then setting up groups in New York, Chicago, and Boston. Gurdjieff was outraged at being abandoned by Ouspensky and his English group, although he in part at least had himself to thank, already having badly wounded this aristocratic mathematician-thinker back in Essentuki in 1918 by the incomprehensible 'artistry' with which he managed to alienate the most loyal disciples: Ouspensky logically began reasoning that there might be more than one way and one man for putting the priceless teachings of the Masters of Wisdom into practice.

Indeed Ouspensky, a dry, precise, and somewhat humorless intellectual whose one fatal limitation was the inability to see beyond the psychic domain, was except for this limitation the very antithesis of his Rabelaisian guru, who modelled himself after the fabulous Mullah Nassr Eddin. He nevertheless visited Fontainebleau from time to time in an effort to maintain harmony between the two groups; and it was only when Gurdjieff sailed for America that the rupture—possibly provoked by money matters—became established. Just before this, Winifred Alice Beaumont (soon to marry Bennett) had interrogated Ouspensky: 'I want you to tell me the truth about Gurdjieff. I know he is not an ordinary man, but I cannot tell if he is very good or very bad,' and the immediate reply was: 'I can assure you that Gurdjieff is a good man.' Yet by the time of the auto crash, Ouspensky was warning that Gurdjieff had two 'I's,

> one very good and one very bad. I believe that in the end the good 'I' will conquer. But meanwhile it is very dangerous to be near him. . . . He could go mad. Or else he could attract to

himself some disaster in which all those round him would be involved.

This hardly coheres with Bennett's assertion that Gurdjieff achieved 'liberation from the "pairs of opposites"' in his thirty-second year, but it certainly tallies with the account given by Peters, who says

> he frequently warned that his work could only become more difficult as one learned more; in other words, as one grew one did not achieve any greater peace or any visible, or tangible reward- one did not become obviously 'good'—but the struggle between any individual's capacity for 'good' or 'evil' for himself became that much more intensified. Mr Gurdjieff himself, was an interesting example of this particular theory and I often thought that his personal power was such that he could very easily do as much harm as he could do good.

Fritz Peters' word particularly merits attention, because he not only reports with artless candor and shattering honesty, but in addition he is about as impartial and 'neutral' a witness as might be found among the biographers who knew Gurdjieff personally, being neither strictly a disciple and therefore a proponent 'committed' to the message, nor someone disaffected by the movement and out to blacken its leader. He was practically speaking a child of circumstance, raised like an orphan at the Prieuré, with no special regard for the teachings, and simply the attachment or 'very great, genuine affection' for Gurdjieff that a child feels towards a parent. But he is the first to admit that his involuntary involvement precludes total objectivity, especially as Gurdjieff claimed to have put something into him as a boy that went considerably deeper than what a mere pupil might acquire:

> You learn in skin, and you cannot escape.... I already in your blood—make your life miserable for ever—but such misery can be good thing for your soul, so even when miserable you must thank your God for suffering I give you.

Apparently Gurdjieff became sufficiently convinced that Peters was 'poisoned for life' to qualify for successor, since he was publicly thus designated, in 1945. This must not be taken too seriously, as Bennett was likewise a recipient of the same honour during a private talk with Gurdjieff at his cafe on the Avenue des Ternes ('Only you can repay for all my labors'); and goodness knows on to how many other shoulders the mantle passed, although Bennett was doubtless the last to receive it, as Gurdjieff died a week later. Peters assessed the imponderables of his 'election' very astutely:

> (1) 'It was actually true' (although 'I did not honestly know in what his "work" consisted'); (2) 'It was intended to "expose" my ego to myself.' (3) 'It was intended to produce various reactions in the other persons present'; (4) 'It was a huge joke on the devout followers.'

While the reader is not told his definitive conclusion if there was one, Peters does indirectly drop a clue in his dual evaluation of Gurdjieff as being 'some sort of self-created, inevitable Messiah,' and 'in a very literal, paradoxical sense, the embodiment of that excellent phrase: "a real, genuine phony"'—two ideas which are less totally contradictory than might at first appear.

✵

Profiting from the insomnia suffered during his convalescence, Gurdjieff, who slept little anyhow, began devising a scheme whereby to disseminate his ideas throughout the world in writing. And thus, over a midnight coffee, with Olga de Hartmann taking the dictation, began *All and Everything: Beelzebub's Tales to His Grandson*: 'It was in the year 223 after the creation of the World,' came the words in Russian. 'Through the Universe flew the ship Karnak of the "trans-space" communication....' Never one to conceive anything on a scale less than Gargantuan, he planned this work exceeding well a thousand pages to be but the first series of a trilogy, whose second part would be the quasi-or-pseudo-autobiographical *Meetings with Remarkable Men*, and the third, *Life is Real Only Then, When 'I Am'*, where his most intimate speculations would be unveiled. When he was later able to write himself, he put down his thoughts in Armenian, which was then translated back by the Armenians into poor Russian and revised by Mme de Hartmann before being translated into dictionary English by her husband and then polished by Orage (who helped set the final idiom) and the English-speaking students. For 'Headquarters' the author chose the Café de la Paix in Paris, although he also wrote in restaurants, 'dance-halls', and other what he calls 'kindred "temples" of contemporary morality.' Then came the shock in 1927: after monitoring frequent public readings of *Beelzebub*, Gurdjieff was forced to register the fact that his listeners could scarce understand a word. Whether the book was too esoteric, or whether his thoughts became hopelessly garbled from the multiple translations, he saw that it would all have to be redone. (Some readers may find the final version equally incoherent, but this is beside the point.)

A decision had to be made. By his calculations the whole work of revision and publication would take some seven years to complete. Yet neither he as experienced diagnostician nor the doctors foresaw the possibility of his being able to outlive even half that span of time. He determined therefore to 'mobilize all capacities', and if no solution were forthcoming by the following New Year (Gurdjieff considered his birthday to be the 1st of January old style), 'then on the evening of the last day of the Old Year to begin to destroy all my writings, calculating the time so that at midnight with the last page to destroy myself also.'

He now began to notice that his literary output or 'laborability' was in direct proportion to the amount of suffering he had to endure, lately intensified by the deaths, first of his mother and then his wife; thus circumstantially the answer to his problem dawned on him at Christmas, that a principle could be established—and eventually applied to others concerning the relationship between intentional suffering (for which he coined the word *partkdolg-duty*, from an amalgam of Armenian, Russian, and English) and creative work—a formula to be immortalized on his mother's tombstone:

Ici repose
La mere de celui
Qui se vit par

Cette mort force
Decrire ce livre
Intitule
Les Opiumistes[12]

It only needed now putting theory into practice, and on the 6th of May 1928 Gurdjieff made an irrevocable oath before his own essence, 'under the pretext of different worthy reasons, to remove from my eyesight all those who by this or that make my life too comfortable.' Since having his friends around was not all that comfortable, for he writes that during his 'Great Illness' they 'came-sucked-me-out-like-vampires-and-went-away,' one has to suppose that not having them around would prove still more uncomfortable. We have already seen how he got rid of Ouspensky. Among his closest and oldest associates next shown the door were Dr Stjernwal, Gurdjieff's right-hand man ever since the founding of the Institute in Russia, with his wife and children; the young Russians Ivanoff and Ferapontoff, respectively leader of the 'movements' demonstrations and personal secretary and translator of the lectures into English—both men wandered off bedazed to Australia; Dr Maurice Nicoll, a leading exponent of Jungian psychology; Orage, who left to become editor of the *New English Weekly*; Alexander de Salzmann, who went to Switzerland where he soon died; Thomas de Hartmann, because conditions were made so unbearable that he was forced out on the verge of a nervous breakdown; and then his wife, because she could not acquiesce to Gurdjieff's demand that

12. Here lies
The mother of him
Who finds himself by
This death compelled
To write this book
Entitled
The Opiumists.

One can wonder that the normal culmination of an aged lady's life could so traumatize her son; the book moreover is not known. Gurdjieff however, was extremely sentimental about family ties—epitaph to the contrary. If this commemoration proves anything, it is that its author lived the contradiction that most biographers feel was opportunistically 'posed'.

her husband now be forced back. Bennett just before this period had found himself maneuvered into a position where there was no alternative but to leave the Prieuré; he managed, however, to rejoin the thaumaturge twenty-five years later. As for Peters, he was told at the time of his investiture never to return; he tried, nevertheless, only to have Gurdjieff close the door in his face with the words: 'Cannot say goodbye again—this already done.' Orage back in the early thirties, having found separation intolerable, made the decision to terminate his activities and return to France; that night he died of heart failure—which hit Gurdjieff with something of a shock. Even Ouspensky around the time of his final illness in 1947 was crying in his cups: 'Doesn't he understand how much I love him? Why does he not let me go back to him? He knows that I need him and I know that he needs me.'

The prognosis established by Gurdjieff and his physicians proved to be way off target, for he was to live well over seven times the number of years allotted. While writing at this period, he also solicited from de Hartmann more than a hundred musical scores as emotive accompaniment to the readings from chapters of *Beelzebub*, which book he managed to rewrite completely within eighteen months. Life at the Prieuré meantime slowly regained its former momentum: for all the people gone, there were always enough new 'calves' around to keep the Institute developing, harmoniously or otherwise. And then there were more trips to America, in 1929, 1930, and right on until the War, mostly spent with his groups in Chicago and particularly New York, where he held 'office' at Child's Restaurant on Fifth Avenue and 56th Street, or one of its branches. Bennett says there are reasons to believe that Gurdjieff also made one or more brief trips to Asia during these years; at least the postmarks on letters received show that he was continuously in touch with Turkestan. And when he spoke of 'writing letters of enquiry to ... friends whom he respected', it was obviously not his pupils that he had in mind.[13]

13. For the sake of the record, one of the 'Seekers of Truth' with Gurdjieff during his early travels in Asia has been identified according to Louis Pauwels on the testimony of the French scientist Jacques Bergier as being Karl Haushofer, a German army officer and geographer of notorious fame, who was not only political

❂

All the tensions and *remue-ménage* in the years following the auto-mobile accident, compounded by financial difficulties, finally forced the closing and selling of the Prieuré, in 1933; and Gurdjieff eventually moved into the Paris apartment of his deceased brother Dimitri, a rather dank and dingy flat at 6 rue des Colonels Renard near the Etoile, which was to remain his residence to the end. Peters observed in 1945 that

> except for the fact that there were no grounds and gardens in which Mr Gurdjieff's students could labor, the 'teaching' of his method did not seem to me to have changed very much. There were still readings, lectures, dance groups, and interviews with particular students. The only thing missing in the general ambi-ence was 'The Prieuré itself'.

He was perpetually busy trying to get his trilogy polished and pub-lished, for although written exclusively for the 'Inner Circle', it was clearly too momentous a work to be forever withheld from human-ity. His life style during those years was to buy food at the market, which he would then prepare, cook, and serve—his tasselled magenta fez replacing the chef's hat—to maybe forty or more peo-ple in a dining room made to hold six, which inevitably left the majority of guests standing wedged in halls and doorways while dishes were relayed from the kitchen at the password: 'Chain!' Some commentators have thought to discern an analogy between these banquets and the Lord's Supper—a proof if nothing else of Gurdji-eff's dictum about the ease with which people by the power of sug-gestion can be made to 'believe any old tale.'

During the war he managed besides his rug trade to harvest pro-ceeds from a company he owned which fabricated false eyelashes;

---

adviser to Hitler but also founder of the secret society, Order of Thule, to which Hitler and other top Nazi officials belonged. The philosophical tenets of this order were drawn from the Tibetan grimoire *Dzyan*. It is claimed that Gurdjieff was in continuous contact with Haushofer, to whom moreover he proposed the emblem of the inverted swastika.

moreover he apparently maintained himself rather handsomely amidst scarcity, for in his words:

I make deal with Germans, with policemen, with all kinds idealistic people who make 'black market'. Result: I eat well and continue have tobacco, liquor, and what is necessary for me and for many others. While I do this—very difficult thing for most people—I also can help many people.

Peters noticed, in fact, that his mentor seemed to support with unwonted deference quite a 'retinue' of old and destitute persons who visited his apartment each day. When not there, he could almost always be found at the Café de la Paix, holding forth like a boulevardier Pythagoras or latter-day Falstaff.

✪

Bennett renewed the contact in the summer of 1948. Just at this time Gurdjieff set off in a borrowed car on one of his motor jaunts, heading for Cannes, when in passing through a small village his car was rammed by a delivery wagon with a drunken driver, who with his passenger was instantly killed; Gurdjieff's three passengers escaped serious injury, but he himself was pinned in the buckled car between the wheel and the seat, from which it took an hour to extricate him. He was perfectly conscious the whole time and directed each movement to prevent fatal loss of blood.

Bennett reached the rue des Colonels Renard the following evening just as two cars drove slowly up. From one of them Gurdjieff painfully emerged, spattered with blood and black with bruises. Bennett realized that he

was looking at a dying man. Even this is not enough to express it. It was a dead man, a corpse, that came out of the car; and yet it walked. I was shivering like someone who sees a ghost.

With iron-like tenacity Gurdjieff managed to gain his room, where he sat down and said: 'Now all organs are destroyed. Must make new.' Then he turned to Bennett, smiling: 'Tonight you come dinner.

I must make body work.' As he spoke a great spasm of pain shook his body and blood gushed from an ear. Bennett thought: 'He has a cerebral hemorrhage. He will kill himself if he continues to force his body to move.' But then he reflected: 'He has to do all this. If he allows his body to stop moving, he will die. He has power over his body.'

Although the doctor once there ordered Gurdjieff immediately to bed on risk of dying of pneumonia if nothing else, his patient disobeyed and came to dinner as usual—fractured skull, smashed ribs, blood—filled lungs, and all—to the indescribable agony of those present. When he did finally go to bed he declined the morphia that had been sent for, saying he had found 'how to live with pain'. He also refused penicillin ('It is poison for the psyche of man') and x-rays, and yet through some incredible deployment of inner energy he knitted together so well again that by two weeks he was back to his habitual routines.

But Gurdjieff must have seen that the moment had come to play his trump card, for he now began gathering in pupils new and old from all over the world. He already told Bennett just three or four days after the accident to bring across his group from England: 'Let all come. . . . Necessary not to lose time.' Thus this notable English scientist, linguist, mathematician, traveller, and seeker urged his followers to place themselves directly under Gurdjieff's guidance:

I now have . . . what I would call *Objective Hope* that I can achieve the transformation of Being that has been my aim for nearly thirty years. I believe that the same objective hope exists for all of you. I must warn you that Gurdjieff is far more of an enigma than you can imagine. I am certain that he is deeply good, and that he is working for the good of mankind. But his methods are often incomprehensible. For example, he uses disgusting language, especially to ladies who are likely to be squeamish about such things. He has the reputation of behaving shamelessly over money matters, and with women also. At his table, we have to drink spirits, often to the point of drunkenness. People have said that he is a magician, and that he uses his powers for his own ends. . . . What I do know is that he can show us the way to work effectively so as to get results . . . by the very simple means of invoking the powers latent in our own bodies.

From my point of view, whatever may be the risk and however great may be the payment, the game is worth the candle.

❂

Every morning, afternoon, evening, and night: rhythmic exercises, readings, private consultations, and Pantagruelian feasts without interruption, plus droves of people all the time arriving; the tension was accumulating until becoming intolerable. What with the battering of egos and general pandemonium, hard-headed business magnates were reduced to weeping, and some men and women after a single week-end with Gurdjieff had to leave for the nearest mental hospital. No matter what went 'wrong', it was always 'right', since all served to further the 'work'.

But Gurdjieff could be extraordinarily courteous when he wished, as Denis Saurat already had the occasion to observe in an interview with him years earlier. Or tender, as, when playing some melancholy Eastern air on his little hand organ at two in the morning until all eyes were moist, he would suddenly stop, intuiting his listeners' thoughts, and after a pause say quietly, 'It is a prayer.' Or disarming, as a timid lady disciple might discover upon ringing his doorbell when he himself answered and she found herself transfixed speechless before a face whose masks for once were gone and which now appeared to radiate nothing but charity for the world; he would calm her with the simple explanation, 'God helps me.'

That autumn the maestro left once more for America, to see his groups and arrange for the publishing of *Beelzebub*. The pattern was always the same: gatherings in Child's restaurant, feasts in his hotel-apartment with music pumped out of the unfailing accordion until about two in the morning, when Gurdjieff would catch some three hours' sleep before a dawn visit to the markets to buy provisions for feeding up to eighty pupils.

Upon Gurdjieff's return to France the following spring at the age of seventy-two his health began deteriorating rapidly; and although he passed the summer in his usual manner, devising all sorts of projects and planning another trip to America, he was mainly preoccupied with how his work would be carried on in the future. 'The next five years will decide,' he said.

It is the beginning of a new world. I must make the old world 'Tchik' [i.e., squash it like a louse], or else it will make me 'Tchik'. From now on, I need soldiers who will fight for me for the new world.

On the 21st of October he saw the proofs of the American edition of *Beelzebub*, and apparently took this as a sign that his work was done, for the next day he went to his cafe for the last time. Gurdjieff's legs were so swollen with dropsy that when he tried to leave, Bennett had to hoist him into the car, which he nevertheless insisted on driving. For Bennett it was a terrifying experience, as Gurdjieff had no strength to apply the brake. After a near collision with a truck the car crazily coasted to a stop at his flat.

Four days later Gurdjieff was carried out on a stretcher and moved to the American Hospital, where he cracked jokes over a cigarette while the doctor tapped his dropsy. 'Bravo America,' he said, and slumped into a coma. At eleven a.m. on the 29th of October, 1949, he was dead.

Or was he? One of his disciples, Solita Solano, wrote: 'Four hours after his death his forehead and neck were still very warm; the doctor said he couldn't understand it.' And Bennett, who arrived on the first plane from England, said after the embalming: 'I was convinced that he was breathing. When I shut my eyes and held my breath I could distinctly hear a regular breathing—although no one else was in the chapel.'

The doctors were even more mystified, after the autopsy showed what a state of deterioration most of Gurdjieff's organs were in, that he had been able to live for so long. The body lay for four days in the mortuary chapel of the hospital, where the disciples kept a permanent day-night vigil amidst a profusion of flowers and throngs of constantly passing visitors. Then the bier was transported to the Russian Cathedral in the rue Darti, where the priest offered a short prayer service. Mme de Hartmann writes:

When the priest finished the ceremony and entered the altar, he closed the curtains. At this moment the electric lights went out . . . for some inexplicable reason [according to the priest]. . . . The church was plunged into darkness, illuminated only by little candles burning before images.

It was Thomas de Hartmann who wrote the eulogy for the burial service, composing it so

that the last words pronounced by the priest in front of Mr Gurdjieff's coffin in the Russian church were words from 'The Struggle of the Magicians'.

Solita Solano reported:

The priest at the Russian church stated that there has never been such a funeral before, except Chaliapin's; that he has never seen such mass grief, or such a concentration of attitude on the part of the mourners. Even the undertaker who had never seen Gurdjieff before he saw him dead, broke down at the grave and wept. just from the vibrations, I daresay.

Gurdjieff was buried in a nameless grave at Avon, which has since become a Mecca of sorts, as Bennett on his Coombe Springs estate near Kingston, Surrey, erected in 1957 a curious nine-sided building designed to concentrate spiritual vibrations, called the Djamichunatra—from a place described in chapter 46 of *All and Everything* where the soul receives 'second being food'—and laid out so that the central axis pointed to Fontainebleau.[14]

---

14. This temple of vibrations was inaugurated upon the arrival of the Indonesian thaumaturge, Pak Subuh, at Coombe Springs, who seemed to be the key to Gurdjieff's enigmatic premonition in May, 1949: 'I need Dutch group, for contact with Dutch India.' Subuh's visit is a story in itself, already much publicized following the sensational cure of the actress Eva Bartok. In one month at Bennett's estate over four hundred people were 'opened' by the mage's *latihan*; and one man in his zeal for progress let his *latihan* get so out of control that he ended up dying on the carpet. It was too much even for Subuh, who exclaimed: 'Bapak has never seen anything like this in twenty-five years.'

2

THE TEACHING

I am not trifling with words when I say that for some writers the Gurdjieff experiment, which is the great temptation, has and still does risk opening the ways to sickness, the hospital bed, and the cemetery.

LOUIS PAUWELS is the author of this admonition, which is quoted from his article 'Une société secrète: les disciples de Georges Gurdjieff', published in the periodical *Arts*, May 1–7, 1952, wherein he assesses his encounter with Gurdjieff during the two years that he worked in a group under the direction of Mme de Salzmann. He goes on to say:

However, thanks to Gurdjieff I received a teaching on the arbitrary mechanism of the mind, on the illusion of living and thinking, on the nonpossession of self, on the phantasmal existence of being and the possibilities of acquiring a real life, which is still today my most precious possession. I think that those who like myself have had the fortune to escape from Gurdjieff and who are serious enough to take true stock of their stay with him, rightly regard themselves as being damaged forever, yet also initiated[1] into the essential weaknesses and strengths of human nature. This is why I cannot speak of him without joining to the simplicities of condemnation the ambiguities of the profoundest respect.

1. Some adepts have called Gurdjieff's transfer of powers an 'initiation into surrealism'.

These observations call for several comments. First: on the basis of the evidence, it is not just writers who have been tempted to the experiment, nor writers alone who have succumbed to the results, the risks being no one's priority. Secondly: few persons could admit that the condemnation pronounced by Pauwels is convincingly counterbalanced by the homage which follows, the permanent damage to which he so candidly testifies being a grave price to pay for any teaching whatever. And others who have tried to dissociate themselves from the movement know only too well that he is not exaggerating—that they really have a monkey on their backs. Thirdly: the insights and acquisitions constituting what Pauwels calls his 'most precious possession' are fully and integrally to be realized in the spiritual practices furnished by every authentic traditional organization, on the one indispensable condition of complete submission to the Divine Will—revealed through the doctrines and rites of the religion in question—under guidance of a qualified master; this possession moreover is not only precious, it is priceless, as it includes everything, against it the gates of hell shall not prevail, and once acquired, it can never be lost.

What then is this patrimony of ancient sages brought to the West by Gurdjieff, this *something extra*, over and above what revealed traditions have to offer, that makes men like Pauwels and Bennett insist that 'the game is worth the candle'? We shall therefore have to scrutinize with some care the teachings conveyed by Gurdjieff and see what is left in the sieve of his vision once all traditional elements have been sifted out. We need not, meanwhile, act unduly deferential towards the term 'ancient sages', which like 'Liberty, Equality, Fraternity' has a ringing catch in the ear and can mean about anything one wishes it to mean. It is not traditional doctrines alone that go back into antiquity: subversive doctrines also claim a pedigree as 'ancient and honourable' as you please.

Gurdjieff envied Ouspensky's abilities as a writer, but no one was his peer when it came to speaking: he could literally magnetize his listeners. Although they came away differing about what precisely had been said, they were in perfect unanimity that whatever it was, it was absolutely phenomenal. Bennett thinks the explanation for this lies in the fact that two different levels of consciousness were involved, with memory unable to provide the link. But this cannot be entirely true, as in a recently published book, *Views from the Real World: Early Talks of Gurdjieff, As Recollected by his Pupils*, those who edited the work claim that 'even in these notes from memory, it is striking that there is always the same human tone of voice, the same man evoking a secret response in each of his listeners.' One could of course rejoin that since much of what Gurdjieff said appears banal enough in print, therefore these words must have conveyed a second meaning on a deeper level of consciousness; yet by this token we have to be equally deferential when confronted, for example, with the inventions of a drug mystic, thus bidding farewell to objective criteria. Gurdjieff, incidentally, did administer drugs on occasion to some of his pupils to get certain psychic results, but this was little compared with the power of his *hanbledzoin*, as explained in the first part of this treatise.

Anyhow, we are not obliged to leave our reasoning suspended in clouds of subjectivity, for Gurdjieff himself gave his imprimatur to Ouspensky's thoroughly documented In Search of the Miraculous, originally called Fragments of an Unknown Teaching. When Bennett read out of this book to him, 'he listened with evident relish, and when I finished he said: 'Before I hate Ouspensky: now I love him. This very exact, he tell what I say.' The information given by other followers also sufficiently concurs with the broad outlines of the exposition presented by Gurdjieff's foremost Russian disciple to make it perfectly clear that the corpus of teachings at our disposal is authentically what the Armenian thaumaturge expounded.

The focal point of Gurdjieff's message lies in the famous injunction: 'Know thyself' — an exhortation that traditionally has two poles. On the one hand we are enjoined by spiritual authorities to know our individual self in all its potentialities, pretensions, and limitations; and on the other we are to know our true Self, the one real Being sustaining all separate selves behind their illusory independence. This doctrine, of course, is universal, and given great prominence, for example, in Buddhism. Since the Yesevi order of Sufis has been mentioned, it is fitting to cite in this context (from Bennett) several beautiful precepts of a twelfth-century Bokharan Sufi in the same spiritual lineage, named Abdulhalik Gujduvani:

Be present at every breath. Do not let thy attention wander for
the duration of a single breath. Remember thyself always and in
all situations
Thy journey is towards thy homeland. Remember that thou art
travelling from the world of appearances to the World of Reality.
Solitude in the crowd. In all thy outward activity remain inwardly
free. Learn not to identify thyself with anything whatsoever.
Remember thy Friend (Allāh). Let the invocation (*dhikr*) of thy
tongue be the invocation of thy heart (*qalb*).
Be constantly aware of the quality of the Divine Presence.
Become used to recognizing the Presence of Allah in thy heart.

How does Gurdjieff expound this message? Man, he says, is born
without a soul; the soul can only be acquired through conscious
effort. Ordinary people are just machines, no better than fertilizer—
and to make sure his listeners got the point, he used the four-letter
word for it (or five when speaking French) in his inimitable English,
which is mentioned here on purpose—not out of derision for any
failure on his part to master all the intricacies of English or French,
which would be ridiculous—but because, although no mean linguist and philologist, he nevertheless deliberately exploited barbar-
isms for calculated effect: 'When he spoke or lectured,' says Bennett,
'he paid no attention to the rules of grammar, logic or consistency;
[he] went further and put all rules behind him.'

To continue: we are so far in the school of Leucippus and Democritus, who taught that a soul can be acquired; but Gurdjieff unlike
Democritus does allow that a soul upon a certain degree of development can survive physical death—at least in some measure. What he
further has to say about immortality, 'reincarnation', an 'astral body',
and the rest is too chaotic to assemble into a rational formulation.
From the traditional perspective, a person without a soul is as
unthinkable as a body without a heart, a square circle, dry water, or
a tree minus roots, since the body is purely the projection or 'outer
shell' of the soul.

Anyway, Gurdjieff tells us that people have the illusion of being
conscious when in reality they are asleep, essentially unconscious,
with no true self or identity which they can call their own. But the

possibility exists of acquiring a real consciousness, a volition under control, and a permanent *individuality*. Only, to achieve this, one must die to what one presently is. Yet in order to die, and not just 'perish like dogs' the way ordinary mortals do, we must first wake up to the mess we are in; when this is recognized and admitted, then we are ready to pass through death and rebirth into true 'being'. The way is by voluntary suffering (if we can overlook the fact that we have no volition) and strenuous effort; it is in Gurdjieff's words *a way against nature, against God*. Hypnosis applied to what he calls our 'personality', namely, the accidents and blind accretions making up our life, can help in the liberation of what he calls our 'essence', namely, the *individuality* in its raw untrammeled state. Since man at the start *is not*, there can be no question, for a 'nonentity' joining the Gurdjieff group, of making agreements or assuming obligations; he is not in any position to undertake a pact or receive an initiation, the only initiation being 'self-initiation'—a concept which Mme De Hartmann, and doubtless many others, found particularly appealing.

Although the brain for Gurdjieff 'is just a muscle', man has three of these 'muscles', being a 'three-brained' creature, in contradistinction to two-brained vertebrates and one-brained invertebrates. Formerly these three interrelated faculties functioned harmoniously as a single co-ordinate, controlling simultaneously the 'motor' or instinctive center in man, the 'emotional' center, and the mental or 'intellectual' center; but some four thousand five hundred years ago there occurred a split in the psyche which fouled up the contact between centers, and rendered them 'completely independent "entities", which bear no relation to each other', thus hobbling the normal course of man's 'evolution'. Hence, writes Gurdjieff in *The Herald of Coming Good*,

> it has come about that a modern man represents three different men in a single individual; the first of whom thinks in complete isolation from the other parts, the second merely feels, and the third acts only automatically.

These categories call to mind Dr William Sheldon's classification of human patterns into what he called the three physical components of mesomorphy, endomorphy, and ectomorphy, with the accompanying psychological characteristics respectively of somatotonic, viscerotonic, and cerebrotonic man. Gurdjieff held in particular disdain the 'cerebrotonic' or 'intellectual' type as exemplified by the 'absent-minded professor', and he seemed to relish putting such people to work at Fontainebleau digging enormous ditches, which he would have them fill back in the following morning; or again, getting middle-aged English ladies to grub up the roots of huge trees felled by the men, which they would despairingly attack with trowels or even tablespoons where only winches would suffice, throwing little heaps of earth behind them while glancing surreptitiously from time to time at papers tucked under sleeves and bracelets scrawled with long lists of Tibetan words they had been charged to memorize.[2]

Sometimes Gurdjieff spoke of these three types in terms of the fakir, the monk, and the yogi, all of whom, unlike the educated European who with his 'exact knowledge' and belief in progress and culture is making no progress at all, are in their crude, blundering manner at least on the way to evolution. The worst blunderers are the fakirs, namely those who struggling to gain power over the body submit themselves to terrible sufferings and tortures for a pittance of results blindly acquired; the monk is a bit smarter about knowing what he wants and, with the feeling that his efforts and sacrifices are 'pleasing to God', can get in a week what the fakir needs a month to obtain; the yogi is the most sophisticated of the three, knowing very well what he wants and how to go about getting it; he can in a day cover a week's work of the monk. But these three ways alike require the renunciation of all worldly ties in return for very partial results

---

2. A concert pianist infatuated with his beautiful hands was put in care of the poultry. After a time he nervously confided to Gurdjieff that the hens are not laying well. 'Of course not,' came the reply, 'because you not love them. Hens here know people. They lay for people who love them. Must learn to love them. 'Bennett chanced upon the distraught pianist at the henhouse the next day, struggling to carry out orders, but clearly bewildered as to how to win a hen's heart.... The mage's defenders claim that these people had only themselves to thank for their lack of critical faculties. This may well be; it was not easy to maintain critical objectivity in his presence.

and hence are ultimately unsatisfactory. Thus in one stroke do we see the likes of Rumi, St Francis of Assisi, and Shankarâchârya eliminated unless one replies that they were secret practitioners of the Fourth Way.

This Fourth Way, which is the most difficult to find because it is very little known and has more or less to be stumbled upon, is at the same time the easiest to follow, since it dispenses with the clutter of religion and everything 'superfluous' 'preserved' by 'tradition'; it requires no retirement into the desert and yet can work in the aforementioned three directions simultaneously simply by the preparation and swallowing of 'a little pill which contains all the substances.' For this reason it

> is sometimes called *the way of the sly man*. The 'sly man' knows some secret which the fakir, monk, and yogi do not know. How the 'sly man' learned this secret—it is not known. Perhaps he found it in some old books, perhaps he inherited it, perhaps he bought it, perhaps he stole it from someone. It makes no difference. The 'sly man' knows the secret and with its help outstrips the fakir, the monk, and the yogi.

The source for this teaching is from the Sarmoun Brethren of Babylon, which, whatever else may be intended here, is almost certainly an alias of Georgi Ivanovitch Gurdjieff.

On occasion the schema was amplified to include seven Mithraic-like categories, *man number five* possessing a knowledge even more objective than what is known by man number four, while *man number six* has complete knowledge. But he can still lose it; *man number seven* alone enjoys 'the *objective* and completely *practical* knowledge of *All*.'

❂

On the subject of knowledge, Gurdjieff taught that it is *material*, hence possessing all the characteristics of materiality. Like 'the sand of the desert and the water of the sea [there] is a definite and unchangeable quantity,' so that the more you have here the less you have there. This means that if knowledge were evenly apportioned among the masses, it would become so diluted that no one would be a jot wiser, but everybody definitely dumber, not to say worse. Whereas if the limited reserves of this knowledge are concentrated with a few highly chosen initiates, they will be tremendously wise and of enormous benefit to humanity, the vast majority of people being in any case too stupid to want knowledge, let alone to know they even lack it. From the traditional viewpoint, Pure Knowledge, being an attribute of Divinity, is Infinite—hence inexhaustible—and no more 'partitionable' than Pure Being or Pure Beatitude. It is God's gnosis that 'measures' the world, and not vice versa.

Nor is knowledge for Gurdjieff the only ponderable imponderable; 'everything in the Universe is material':

the Absolute is as material, as weighable and measurable, as the moon, or as man. If the absolute is God it means that God can be weighed and measured, resolved into component elements, 'calculated', and expressed in the form of a definite formula. . . . *Therefore the Great Knowledge is more materialistic than materialism.* . . . I repeat: everything in the Universe is material. Ponder these words and you will understand, at least to some degree, why I used the expression '*more materialistic than materialism*'. . . . God and microbe are the same system, the only difference is in the number of centers.

We are back again with Democritus—unless the 'ancient sages' drawn upon here were others like Châravâka of the nâstikas in India, or Pakudha Kachchâyana, the hump-backed philosopher of the Âjîvika sect, who lived in the fifth century BC.

It must be clearly understood that what Gurdjieff teaches cosmologically is a form of atomism; and it must be equally well understood that not a trace of atomism is to be found in any of the great traditional systems either Eastern or Western, this tenet—apart from the variations advanced by one or two modern philosophical schools—turning up uniquely in certain heretical pockets on the fringes of these traditions.

The world, he states, is composed of vibrating matter, the rate of vibration being in inverse ratio to the density of matter. 'In the

Absolute vibrations are the most rapid and matter is the least dense. In the next world vibrations are slower and matter denser; and further on matter is still more dense and vibrations correspondingly slower.'

The 'Absolute' can be called world 1, whose atoms alone are really 'indivisible'. Through the intervention of an active, passive, and neutralizing principle, the 'Absolute' begets a trinity, or world 3, called 'all worlds', whose atoms consist of three atoms of the 'Absolute', being three times bigger and three times heavier, with movements that are correspondingly slower. Next comes world 6, called 'all suns', and which is our Milky Way, the domain of 'archangels'; its atom is six of the 'Absolute' merged together. Then comes world 12, the 'sun', with an atom consisting of twelve primordial particles. The following world by the same progression is number 24, or 'all planets' in our solar system, and is the domain of 'angels'. After this comes the 'earth', world 48. The final world is the 'moon', with an enormous atom of 96 parts, very little movement, and extreme density. This 'moon' is the 'outer darkness' of Gurdjieff's cosmology: it feeds and fattens on the earth's organic life like a 'huge electromagnet that is sucking out its vitality.' But 'in the economy of the universe nothing is lost, and a certain energy having finished its work on one plane goes to another.' Thus the moon, being energized by the forces which death on earth releases, energizes in its turn the whole of terrestrial life. All men are dominated by the moon, save— need it be said?—those who, following the techniques outlined by Gurdjieff, have been able to develop their 'common presence'.

In a similar descending schema starting again with the 'Absolute', these 'worlds' are sometimes designated respectively as the *Protocosmos*, *Ayocosmos* or *Megalocosmos*, *Macrocosmos*, *Deuterocosmos*, *Mesocosmos*, *Tritocosmos* ('man' here replacing the 'earth'), and *Microcosmos* (the 'atom' here replacing the 'moon').

We are now ready to grapple with the question of 'influences' operating throughout the different worlds, which brings up the 'law of three and then, further, still another fundamental law, the Law of Seven, or the *law of octaves*'—also called the Law of Sevenfoldness, or Law of Heptaparaparshinokh. It has already been seen how the 'simultaneous action of three forces'—the positive, the negative, and the neutralizing—is necessary to actualize phenomena; this is the *law of three*. And the perspicacious reader may by now have guessed that the seven worlds outlined above provide the basis for the *law of seven* or the *law of octaves*. All that is required is to identify the 'Absolute' with the musical notation *do*, and we have our scale. Since there is nothing beyond or 'beneath' the 'moon' except the 'Absolute', one can start 'beneath' the 'moon' with *do*, the 'moon' then being *re*, the 'earth' *mi*, 'all planets' *fa*, and so on back to the 'Absolute' *do* which is 'above' 'all worlds'. This only gets a bit involved when Gurdjieff advances the theory of 'inner vibrations', namely, the indefinite number of 'inner octaves' that can be resolved from the fundamental octave. Since each 'world' while having its particular 'vibration' is at the same time permeated with the 'substances' or 'vibrations' of the 'worlds' above it, and since thanks to Gurdjieff's 'discovery' of the role of *hazard*, which does not enter into the Pythagorean and Platonic systems, octaves may receive 'additional shocks' at the *mi-fa* and *si-do* divisions when intersecting certain 'intervals', one can develop octaves within octaves within octaves reverberating into the most unforeseen directions *ad infinitum*.[3]

Returning to the *law of three*, 'the note *do* [in the "Absolute"] will be the conductor of the active force, designated by the number 1, while the matter in which this force acts will be (C) carbon.' The note *si* in turn conducts the passive force, number 2, whose matter is 'oxygen' (O). *La* is then the neutralizing factor, number 3, with 'nitrogen' (N) for its matter.

'Carbon', 'oxygen', and 'nitrogen' together will give matter of the fourth order, or 'hydrogen' (H), whose density we will designate by the number 6 (as the sum of 1, 2, 3), that is H6.

The *law of three* allows for a progression of triads of increasing density, or a 'Table of Hydrogens' based on a sesquialteral combination of two and three. Thus, after H6 come H12, H24, H48, H96, H192,

---

3. Those readers desiring a serious work relating musical theory to cosmological laws will find it in Alain Daniélou's *Introduction to the Study of Musical Scales*, London, 1943.

and right on to 'hydrogen' 3072. Food substances pertain to the density of 'hydrogen' 768; wood, H1536; water, H384, 'Hydrogen' 12 corresponds to the hydrogen of chemistry (atomic weight 1). Gurdjieff goes on to observe that the atomic weights of those elements related to his 'hydrogens' 'stand almost in the correct octave ratio to one another'.

> The 'table of hydrogens' makes it possible to examine all substances making up man's organism from the point of view of their relation to different planes of the universe. And as every function of man is a result of the action of definite substances, and as each substance is connected with a definite plane in the universe, this fact enables us to establish the relation between man's functions and the planes of the universe.

The rarefied 'hydrogens' 48, 24, 12, and 6 are inaccessible to physics and chemistry, being the 'matters of our psychic and spiritual life.' Thus for example, man's thinking center works with 'hydrogen' 48, the motor center with the even faster and more mobile 'hydrogen' 24, and the emotional center with 'hydrogen' 12—which is why the emotional center is so chaotic with most people, this fine 'hydrogen' being beyond their control. And matters are further complicated by the fact that there is a still higher 'thinking center', working with 'hydrogen' 6; it only manifests at sporadic moments in mystical experiences, ecstatic states, epileptic fits, or drug seizures, although if the 'lower centers' were in order, it should normally function harmoniously.

> What is necessary to understand and what the 'table of hydrogens' helps us to grasp, is the idea of the complete materiality of all the psychic, intellectual, emotional, volitional, and other inner processes, including the most exalted poetic inspirations, religious ecstasies, and mystical revelations.... When the substance [sustaining a process] is exhausted, the process comes to a stop.

✷

All these cosmological considerations, as we shall see, absolutely have to be mastered if one is to understand the 'movements' of the 'sacred dances'. The reader who does not wish to master them need nevertheless not throw up his hands in despair, for he can be perfectly assured that all the foregoing exposition is pure Gurdjieff, which while it may make for superb science fiction, is good for little else. And he himself was the first to play down the importance of numerical systems with the comment:

> Mathematik, she is useless. You cannot learn laws of World Creation and World Existence by Mathematik. You must only look for Being. When you have Being, you will know all these things, without the need of Mathematik.

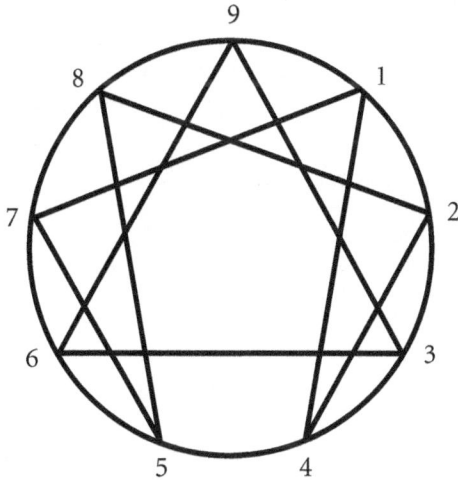

Fascination with magic circles, squares, and numbers was of course another matter, and Gurdjieff's favorite symbol was the Enneagram, a figure composed of a circle divided into nine equal parts connected within by lines forming a triangle interlaced with a twisted hexagon. For him it was a 'universal symbol' of 'perpetual motion'

to which could be appended all his cosmoses, octaves, centers, and 'hydrogens' in every conceivable juxtaposition and variation.

It is true that Gurdjieff draws on elements of traditional doctrine for his own constructions, a fact he sometimes admits and sometimes conceals. He refers to the Kabbalah, for instance, when speaking about the relationship between man and the Universe as being that of the microcosm to the macrocosm; his *law of three* is recognizably related to the *gunas* of Hinduism; and he refers to the famous Emerald Tablet of Hermes for the teaching: 'As above, so below.' The Absolute for him is the primordial All or Whole, from the differentiation of which arises the diversity of phenomena. But his teachings fall within the *guna* of *tamas*, since everything is interpreted from a quantitative, materialistic, and non-transcendent perspective.

The Emerald Tablet in his case is a matter of: 'As below, so beneath,' seeing that he never gets off the ground save to descend into the subconscious. In other words, the only 'worlds' open to his consciousness are the corporeal domain and the lower reaches of the psychic realm. The supraformal, noumenal, or archetypal spheres of reality—namely, everything spiritual—are completely sealed off from his 'common presence'—not to speak of principial Existence itself, and above all the Absolute.

❂

Gurdjieff's attitude toward religion was: respect all faiths—and leave them a wide berth. Peters writes that 'he dismissed all existing religions, philosophies and other systems of thought—as *practiced*— as being worthless.' The preamble to *Beelzebub*, it is true, launches out with the stentorian blast: 'In the name of the Father and of the Son and in the name of the Holy Ghost. Amen.' But the unsuspecting reader is brought down with a thump a few lines later where the author, having made obeisance 'to the notions of religious morality existing among contemporary people,' prides himself as 'beyond all doubt assured that everything further in this new venture of mine will now proceed, as is said, "like a pianola".' And what matters is anyhow the personage honoured in the title of the book, which Gurdjieff himself concedes is a stratagem to secure the fellow's patronage: 'Mr Beelzebub also must possess a good share of vanity, and will therefore find it extremely inconvenient not to help one who is going to advertise His [*sic*] name.'

The founders of the great religions—men like Moses, Jesus, Buddha, and Muhammad—might indeed, we are told, be number eight men, i.e., Cosmic Individuals incarnated from Above; but their 'three-brained' followers invariably made a hash of their teachings, inventing such 'maleficent' notions as—Good and Evil', 'Paradise and Hell', and other misleading 'fantasies'. These 'founders', incidentally, did not reveal; they 'created' religions. One of the great features of Islam for Gurdjieff is the stress on ablution and circumcision, and he devotes thirty-six pages in praise of these 'beneficial customs' as impediments to venereal disease and onanism.

He taught that an ordinary man, not yet being responsible and his own master, can no more be a Christian than can any other 'machine', like a motorcar or gramophone. But 'The Institute can help a man to be able to be a Christian,' and 'this is esoteric Christianity.'

His 'esoteric Christianity' had some strange tenets. Take for example that on the Eucharist:

> The Last Supper was a *magical ceremony* similar to 'blood-brotherhood' for establishing a connection between 'astral bodies'. But who is there who knows about this in existing religions and who understands what it means? All this has long been forgotten and everything has been given quite a different meaning. The words have remained but their meaning has long been lost.

'Holy Writ,' he contends, became completely distorted through the 'criminal wiseacring' of the 'elders of the church'. An illustration of this is the anathema they heap on Judas, who for Gurdjieff is 'now a Saint.' 'Judas,' as Bennett recounts it from *Beelzebub* and from personal conversations,

> was the best and closest friend of Jesus. Judas alone understood why Jesus was on earth. Judas had saved the work of Jesus from

being destroyed, and by his action had made the life of humanity more or less tolerable for two thousand years.[4]

Although this particular perversion of sacred history did not originate with Gurdjieff, he may perfectly well have come by it without the collaboration of 'ancient sages', as it fits like a glove with his 'doctrine' of the necessity of a 'reminding-factor', exposed earlier in this monograph: just as 'God' was compelled to send 'one of His Beloved Sons', namely the 'Devil', into the world for a perpetual 'reminding-factor', so by the same token would Jesus logically be compelled to use his 'best and closest friend,' namely Judas, for the same end.

What did Gurdjieff understand by 'God'? 'Nothing is immortal,' he taught:

> even God is mortal. But there is a great difference between man and God, and, of course, God is mortal in a different way to man. It would be much better if for the word 'immortality' we substitute the words *'existence* after death'.

To get this idea across he used such expressions as: 'OUR COMMON CREATOR, ALMIGHTY AUTOCRAT ENDLESSNESS,' or 'OUR COMMON ALL-EMBRACING UNI-BEING AUTOCRAT ENDLESSNESS.' But the Deity conventionally worshipped in church he referred to as 'Mister God'. For the rest, he compared his relationship to God on somewhat the same terms which a rather independent, obstinate, and touchy minister has with his king.

When questioned, 'In what way does your system differ from the philosophy of the yogis?' Gurdjieff replied:

> Yogis are idealists; we are materialists. I am a skeptic. The first injunction inscribed on the walls of the Institute is: 'Believe nothing, not even yourself.' I believe only if I have obtained the

---

4. He also said: 'Judas is universal type: he can enter into all situations—but he has no type of his own.' Were Gurdjieff a Christian theologian, he would be right on center here, for evil has no reality properly speaking of its own, but attaches like a shadow to the obscure side of manifestation with the 'gravity' or suction of its own voidness.

same results over and over again. I study, I work for guidance, not for belief.

✪

Allusion has already been made to various techniques employed by Gurdjieff to knock people out of their complacency in view of awakening different centers of consciousness hitherto unsuspected in their psyches. He taught certain procedures for fasting, he sometimes used drugs, and there was the constant stress on 'intentional suffering' (*partkdolg-duty*), or exploiting the potential of 'additional shocks' in the system of octaves to boost one's 'consciousness-factor'.

By performing 'sacred gymnastics' based on 'ancient temple dances' from the East of 'religious, mystic, and scientific' significance, his pupils were supposed to acquire a mastery over themselves coupled with universal insights. The 'movements' could become alarmingly complicated, the left arm perhaps moving to the *law of three* while the right traced out the 'Law of Sevenfoldness' with the feet simultaneously measuring sequences of the Enneagram. No sooner did the students gain command of a movement than it might be abandoned for a whole new series. Any beauty the dances had was purely secondary, and Gurdjieff would also teach ugly and discordant movements to liberate his pupils from 'obsession' with their own appearance. Here the women often chafed, finding it repellent to make ugly faces, even if they knew they were there for their psychic development and not just to be admired.

Surveying all this in a black leotard and astrakhan hat, Gurdjieff would suddenly shout: 'Stop!' and the dancers would freeze in whatever stance they happened to find themselves, wobbling to a halt or lunging off balance to the floor like a clutter of abandoned puppets until reanimated some five seconds if not ten minutes later with the shout '*Davay!*' or, 'Continue!'

This famous Stop Exercise was, moreover, something that could happen at any moment, day or night, with the intention of trapping the ego off-guard in a still-life caricature of its habitual smugness for the victim's edification.

Gurdjieff recounts how he and some comrades were once pitch-
ing a tent in Central Asia by an *arik*, or irrigation canal, when a voice
from the tent called 'Stop!' just as one of the men was in the canal
retrieving a fallen axe. At the same moment a farmer a mile away
opened a sluice that rapidly raised the water level. Soon the man was
completely submerged, yet no one could move, shout, or even look
to see if the person in the tent knew what was happening. After what
seemed ages came the cry: 'Enough!' and the men on the bank
sprang into the canal to drag out their half-drowned companion.

All this is a far remove from the ritual cessation of movement
practiced in dances like those of the Mevlevi Dervishes and the
American Indians, where the flutes, the singing, and the drums
unexpectedly stop on an explosion of sound between two instants,
and the dance evaporates into the Void. It is the moment of death,
the close of the cosmic cycle. 'This world is a playground,' says
Rûmî, 'and death is the night.' Or as the *Srimad Bhagavatam*
expresses it: 'My play here is finished. My kingdom is established.'
Then the music resumes, and the Cosmic Wheel turns once again.
'God hath men who enter Paradise through their flutes and drums,'
to cite a saying of Muhammad.

Gurdjieff also gave his pupils various breathing exercises, combined sometimes with mantras. Thus, a person might be required to
sit on the ground with knees bent and hands pressed together
between the feet, then, lifting one leg, to pronounce *Om* ten times
to special measures of breathing while 'sensing' his right eye. Next,
Om had to be repeated nine times, then eight, and so down to one,
after which the series remounted back to ten while the adept sepa-
rated his thumbs and 'sensed' the left ear; the combinations and
complications were interminable, all the different organs, limbs,
muscles, and bones of the body consecutively being fixed upon in
what was called the 'Sensation Exercise'. To keep the mind meanwhile from growing idle, it was put through numerical gymnastics
in the form of $2 \times 1 = 6, 2 \times 2 = 12, 2 \times 3 = 22, 2 \times 4 = 40, 2 \times 5 = 74$
(resolved by adding the sequential progression 4, 8, 16, etc.), or fol-
lowing another system, $2 \times 2 = 1, 4 \times 4 = 13, 5 \times 5 = 28$—done rapidly
to musical accompaniment, and then inversely. If a student fell into
despair, Gurdjieff would reply, 'I am only here for the desperate.'

✿

While the reader sifting through these teachings may well for all his diligence fail to discover something real that is lacking to Tradition, he certainly cannot complain to any paucity of things bizarre. Consider, for example, the so-called 'buffer-of-prejudice': through a strange twist on the doctrine of the Fall, Gurdjieff would have us believe that at some unpredetermined date in history, the 'Higher Powers' felt man's 'evolution' was getting out of hand through more objectivity in his growing consciousness than they were able to cope with; therefore they commissioned the 'Chief-Common-Universal-Arch-Chemist-Physicist Angel Looisos' to plant an organ at the base of the spinal column where this 'three-brained being' still possessed a tail, as a 'buffer' to the 'arising' in him of 'Objective Conscience', which said organ was given the name of 'Kundabuffer', and which acted efficaciously to make men 'perceive reality topsy-turvy,' and to 'engender factors for evoking in them sensations of "pleasure" and "enjoyment".' When it was perceived that the planting of this organ had achieved its desired effect, the 'Higher Powers' ordered it removed; but what they had not perceived—'OUR ENDLESS END-LESSNESS' for all his interminability being in the Gurdjieffian system neither Omnipotent nor Omniscient—was the maleficent repercussions its former presence would continue to exert on succeeding generations. Thus men have persisted from that time until this very day as vain, conceited, and egotistical 'three-brained freaks', where 'everybody talks as if our learned know that half a hundred is fifty'—to quote some words that Gurdjieff puts into the mouth of his 'highly esteemed Mullah Nassr Eddin.' The fact would remain, however, that 'Objective-Conscience' has not entirely disappeared from the scene; indeed in a near primordial state it apparently still lies embedded in the 'subconsciousness', and needs only hypnotism to pry it forth.

The author of these assertions based them on distortions of the *kuṇḍalinī* doctrine, learned no doubt from Theosophical circles, which he held in contempt. By *kuṇḍalinī* the Hindus understand the cosmic energy latent in man, the Shakti or Devi symbolically coiled in the *mūlādhāra* plexus at the base of the spine, and which when awakened by the *prāna* (vital breath) of the *sādhaka* (aspirant) being directed upon it through appropriate yogic techniques under a guru's guidance, mounts the *sushumṇā* column 'situated' within the cerebro-spinal axis, illuminating various *chakras* ('lotuses') or subtle centers in the person, the ultimate aim being deliverance (*moksha*) once this resonance has attained the synthesis of centers—the *sahas-rāra* or 'lotus of a thousand petals', 'situated' at the crown of the head.

When Gurdjieff warns that the *kuṇḍalinī* is 'a very dangerous and terrible thing', the Hindus would be in complete agreement, as its evocation brings into play cosmic powers of the subtle order that can destroy the unwary adept physically, psychically, and spiritually, even leading to demonic states, and can therefore be undertaken only by orthodox Hindus endeavouring to obtain liberation with the aid of competent supervision; but they would be incredulous to hear him tell why he considers it 'dangerous':

Kundalini is not anything desirable or useful for man's development.... In reality [it] is the power of imagination, the power of fantasy, *which takes the place of a real function.* When a man dreams instead of acting, when his dreams take the place of reality, when a man imagines himself to be an eagle, a lion, or a magician, it is the force of Kundalini acting in him. Kundalini can act in all centers and with its help all the centers can be satisfied with the imaginary instead of the real. A sheep which considers itself a lion or a magician lives under the power of Kundalini. Kundalini is a force put into men in order to keep them in their present state. If men could really see their true position and could understand all the horror of it, they would be unable to remain where they are even for one second.[5] They would begin to seek a way out and they would quickly find it, *because there is a way out*; but men fail to see it simply because they are hypnotized. Kundalini is the force that keeps them in a hypnotic state....

5. Which is exactly why Hindus practice *kuṇḍalinī* yoga.

And if . . . a man has heard anything about objective characteristics, Kundalini at once transforms it all into imagination and dreams.

✿

In *Meetings with Remarkable Men*, Gurdjieff records an admonition he received from a venerable Persian dervish:

Let God kill him who himself does not know and yet presumes to show others the way to the doors of His Kingdom.

3

The Phenomenon

THERE is an Eastern tale which speaks about a very rich magician who had a great many sheep. But at the same time this magician was very mean. He did not want to hire shepherds, nor did he want to erect a fence about the pasture where his sheep were grazing. The sheep consequently often wandered into the forest, fell into ravines, and so on, and above all they ran away, for they knew that the magician wanted their flesh and skins and this they did not like.

At last the magician found a remedy. He hypnotized his sheep and suggested to them first of all that they were immortal and that no harm was being done to them when they were skinned, that, on the contrary, it would be very good for them and even pleasant; secondly he suggested that the magician was a good master who loved his flock so much that he was ready to do anything in the world for them; and in the third place he suggested to them that if anything at all were going to happen to them it was not going to happen just then, at any rate not that day, and therefore they had no need to think about it. Further the magician suggested to his sheep that they were not sheep at all; to some of them he suggested that they were lions, to others that they were eagles, to others that they were men, and to others that they were magicians.

And after this all his cares and worries about the sheep came to an end. They never ran away again but quietly awaited the time when the magician would require their flesh and skins.

This tale is a very good illustration of man's position.

Particularly if 'man' here stands for the disciples of the magician who told this tale, namely, Gurdjieff.

❂

In *The Verdict of Bridlegoose*, Llewelyn Powys describes his visit to the theatre in New York in 1924 where the 'dance movements' were being performed. He was able to observe Gurdjieff, who stood smoking near the entrance. The impression Powys had was of a horse jobber, with an indefinable something else which strangely affected the nerves. This feeling was heightened when the pupils came on stage like a warren of rabbits hypnotized under the gaze of a master charlatan. Other spectators with whom Powys talked compared the dancers to frightened mice.

Another British author, Rom Landau, relates in his book *God is My Adventure* an encounter he had with the thaumaturge in the latter's New York hotel room in the early thirties. Explaining that he himself is not at all telepathic, given to mediumship, or subject to hypnotism, Landau says that he nevertheless took the precaution to fix his attention on a young man monitoring the meeting, in order to avoid the 'flame' emanating from his host's eyes. To no avail. In a few seconds he felt his body from the waist down penetrated with a growing weakness enough to render him incapable of leaving his chair had he tried. Only by mustering all his concentration in talk with the young attendant did he finally manage to extricate himself from this 'magic circle'. Upon departing he was presented by Gurdjieff with a copy of his *Herald of Coming Good*; it was bound in imitation suede but of a grain so abrasive it made his teeth grind at the very touch. Landau realized that this was all part of an effect deliberately calculated by the author—whose book reads, moreover, as though conceived in clouds of armagnac (the opening sentence alone, by Landau's count, contains not less than two hundred and eighty four words).

In an anonymous tract, 'Glimpses of Truth', which gives the earliest known report of Gurdjieff and his teachings as encountered near Moscow in 1914, the author writes:

His eyes particularly attracted my attention, not so much in themselves as by the way he looked at me when he greeted me, not as if he saw me for the first time but as though he had known me long and well.

Ouspensky describing his first meeting writes of those 'piercing eyes,' while de Hartmann for his part was right away struck by the man with 'those eyes' . . . of unusual depth and penetration. The word 'beautiful' would hardly be appropriate, but I will say that until that moment I had never seen such eyes nor felt such a look.

Solita Solano spoke of 'this "strange" écru man about whom I could see nothing extraordinary except the size and power of his eyes.' Bennett called them

> the strangest eyes I have ever seen. The two eyes were so different that I wondered if the light had played some trick on me. But Mrs. Beaumont afterwards made the same remark, and added that the difference was in the expression and not in any kind of cast or defect in either eye.

A random look at the photographs of the man in question does indeed show a marked dissymmetry between the eyes, that is, the upturned gaze of each follows a distinctly different axis—a trait characteristic in pathological personalities, although the inverse does not hold, as this idiosyncrasy may have purely physical causes with no ulterior connotations. It is, however, significant to hear Gurdjieff speak in his preamble to *Beelzebub* of 'my peculiar psyche,' and of 'my brain—which is for me, constructed unsuccessfully to the point of mockery. . . .'

These eyes, then, betoken a magnetic personality without for that necessarily being the direct instrument or vehicle of hypnosis, which rather was produced by a psychic power operating on the sanguinary system—if the claims of *Beelzebub's* protagonist can be considered as really referring to his author's own technique:

> I then invented and very soon became expert in . . . a certain hindering of the movement of the blood in certain blood vessels.
> By means of this hindering I obtained the result that although the already mechanized tempo of the blood circulation of their

waking state remained in beings, yet at the same time their real consciousness, that is, the one which they themselves call sub-consciousness, began also to function.

This action on the circulatory system might explain the sensation of weakness experienced by Rom Landau.

Beelzebub with a knowing smile of endearment—horns, tail, hooves, and all—lovingly goes on to tell his grandson, Hassein, how prior to his invention concerning the 'difference-of-the-filling-of-the-blood-vessels,' he had to hypnotize through expenditure of his *hanbledzoin*—a means proving very harmful to his 'being-existence'.

All evidence nonetheless indicates that this mysterious *hanbledzoin* is in fact the hypnotic agent acting on the 'psychic bloodstream' or what Gurdjieff calls the *Inkliazanikshanas* the *Kesdjan body*; therefore one can suppose that a general aura of it was a constant feature of his person, while the deployment which he experienced as harmful only came about at moments of highly concentrated expenditure of this magnetic force.

By way of example, Peters tells how in 1945 in a state of shock and shattered nerves he managed to obtain military leave at Luxembourg to go to Paris, obsessed with the idea of somehow finding Gurdjieff in the war's wake. Summoning the last ounce of energy he finally located the man's address and apartment, where he arrived ready to collapse. Gurdjieff immediately ushered him in, preparing a coffee upon observing his visitor's condition:

> I remember being slumped over the table, sipping at my coffee, when I began to feel a strange uprising of energy within myself— I stared at him, automatically straightened up, and it was as if a violent, electric blue light emanated from him and entered into me. As this happened, I could feel the tiredness drain out of me, but at the same moment his body slumped and his face turned grey as if it was being drained of life.

Gurdjieff excused himself and limped out of the kitchen, only to return some fifteen minutes later

> like a young man again, alert, smiling, sly and full of good spirits. He said that this was a very fortunate meeting, and that while I

had forced him to make an almost impossible effort, it had been—as I had witnessed—a very good thing for both of us.

Bennett underwent a similar experience many years earlier at the Prieuré at a time when his body was racked by chronic dysentery to the point where he could hardly quit his bed. Driven, however 'by a superior Will that was not my own,' he forced himself through some torturous dance exercises 'of incredible complexity,' so exhausting that one pupil after another dropped out:

> Gradually, I became aware that Gurdjieff was putting all his attention on me. . . . Suddenly, I was filled with the influx of an immense power. My body seemed to have turned into light. . . . It was exultation in the faith that can move mountains.

Instead of joining the others for tea, Bennett went digging in the kitchen garden to test this new power. At the end of an hour's furious labor in the fierce heat of the afternoon he still felt no fatigue, and the diarrhoea was gone. He later walked into the forest, where he came upon Gurdjieff and his explanation of this metamorphosis, as being the result of contact with what he calls the 'Higher Emotional Energy':

> There are some people in the world, but they are very rare, who are connected to a Great Reservoir or Accumulator of this energy. This Reservoir has no limits.[1] Those who can draw upon it can be a means of helping others. Suppose that a man needs a hundred units of this energy for his own transformation, but he only has ten units and cannot make more for himself. He is helpless. But with the help of someone who can draw upon the Great Accumulator, he can borrow ninety more. Then his work can be effective. . . . Those who have this quality belong to a special part of the highest caste of humanity.

---

1. Gurdjieff is not being consistent with himself here, because as was demonstrated in the section on the teachings, he considered that *everything* is material, with limitations on the quantity available.

What is he talking about? To situate these remarks, it is necessary to cite the conclusion Guénon draws from his observations on shamanism and sorcery that were summarized in the first part of this study: just as it is known in connection with what is termed 'sacred geography' that sanctuaries, shrines, and places of pilgrimage serve as repositories of spiritual and benefic psychic influences, so inversely is it known concerning cases where the spirituality in centers formerly sacred has become extinct,

> that there are in the world a certain number of 'reservoirs' of [malefic] influences [namely, residual psychic forces of an inferior order], the distribution of which is certainly no matter of chance, serving only too well the designs of the 'powers' responsible for the whole modern deviation,

since they, or more strictly their 'emissaries', know how to conjure up and 'galvanize' these residual energies through a kind of necromancy, in view of exploiting them for subversive ends.

However one turns these words, the essential point is unmistakable: that all extramundane powers of whatever sort are not simply drawn out of empty air but must have one of two sources depending on their nature: either they come from the celestial world as vehicled through authentic, living traditions, or else they come from the nether world as channelled through the fissures left by ancient traditions whether deviated, disintegrating, or already extinct. A seeming ambiguity arises when there is an interpenetration from the two domains, but the determining criterion is given in the Gospel observation: 'He that is not with me is against me.' Guénon adds in what more particularly concerns deviated branches of shamanism, that when the apparent custodians of a tradition from which all spirituality has withdrawn still live on, this confers a far greater vitality to the powers than can be the case with anything emanating from purely 'inanimate' objects.

Now to get back to Gurdjieff no one can dispute that he was born with a charismatic personality; but this does not explain his powers, at the most it only helps explain why he rather than someone else had them. And he certainly did not draw them out of thin air. It would be to disastrously underestimate his character to claim that he indulged in nothing more than humbuggery, and it would be a misappraisement, in Bennett's words,

> to treat him as an isolated phenomenon, unique and self-sufficient. He himself emphatically refuted such suggestions. I have more than once heard him say: 'Every man has a teacher. Even I, Gurdjieff have my teacher.'

It is noteworthy that he never from the time his basic teachings were first known to the end of his life in any manner altered them; and while the reader may be unable to liken the 'epic' *Beelzebub*—the way some people have done—to the *Iliad*, the *Song of Roland*, the *Arabian Nights*, the *Song of Songs*, the *Gospel of Saint John*, the *Mahābhārata*, the *Rāmāyana*, and the *Tao Te Ching*, the fact remains that there is not a sentence inconsistent with the book's overall structure,' a random sampling suffices to show that the vocabulary and technical terms—however outrageous—are always exact within their framework—which is all the more striking, given the distracting conditions in which the opus was written. Gurdjieff in other words did not simply 'chew-the-eraser-on-his-pencil,' as his beloved Mullah Nassr Eddin might have put it; he relayed a 'school' —or anyway a mode—of thought.

We have already seen in the preceding section of this paper that he owed nothing directly to the great orthodox religions of the world, his interest in them at best certainly being no more than cursory; and we have likewise noted in the first section his fascination with the ruins of Babylon and the 'Sarmân Brotherhood', as also with Manichaeism, Mithraism, shamanism, and other decaying elements or extinct relics of 'ancient wisdom'—including something called the 'Imastun Brotherhood' supposedly flourishing seventy generations before the Flood. Beelzebub, incidentally, is depicted as being most ancient and venerable—in keeping with the image which the author strived to convey of his own person.

If, then, it can be admitted that Gurdjieff was a man endowed with a 'mission', and that at the same time he was not delegated by any of the orthodox religions on earth, one is thereby obliged in good faith and logic to seek out the origins of his 'investiture' elsewhere. Now, one mark characterizing the 'residual' nature of his 'ancient sources' is the tenebrous and contradictory quality attaching to his person and teachings, so fugitive that to seize hold is like trying to catch an eel, or grasping at sand.

'Despite our ready response little if any instruction materialized,' wrote Miss Gladys Alexander, a pupil in the early Prieuré days, 'though it was remarkable how the mere prospect of it revived our flagging energies. We lived on anticipation.'

At times Gurdjieff seemed to Peters 'a prophet of doom and disaster and hopelessness,' since he taught that the 'impossible' was the only thing worth attaining; yet 'he nevertheless gave an effect of great encouragement and hope.'

Ouspensky and the Moscow/St Petersburg group were continually baffled by their Master's paradoxical way of erecting a whole cosmological system for them to ponder on, only to abandon it for another equally complicated theory at another session.

One day Gurdjieff set up an entirely new classification of 'hydrogens' according to cosmic traits which was based on an altogether different ratio of octaves than the one the pupils had learned. 'This diagram will not be very comprehensible to you at first,' he said, 'but gradually you will learn to make it out. Only for a long time you will have to take it separately from all the rest.' Adds Ouspensky:

This was in fact all I heard from G. about this strange diagram which actually appeared to upset a great deal of what had been said before.

'The growth of knowledge in one domain evokes the growth of ignorance in another,' taught Gurdjieff, who espoused all dualities, barring uniquely that one basic theological distinction between Good and Evil. And yet *duplicity* was less a feature of his 'being-existence' than *triplicity*, if the 'three-brains' which haunted his 'common presence' for life can be taken as the type of his own brain, 'which is for me,' as he said, 'constructed unsuccessfully to the point of mockery.'

❂

With a perfect disregard for consistency, then, Gurdjieff utilized and vindicated hypnosis as a means of achieving what he called 'Objective Conscience', when he knew full well with one at least of his brains that hypnosis is really a door to narcosis and dreams, as demonstrated in his fable of the magician and the sheep, and in his aspersions on the 'Kundalini'. The way of spiritual realization is anything but passive, and yet Gurdjieff promoted hypnotism as the means of liberating the *subconsciousness*, which he mistakes for the 'real consciousness' whereas in fact it is just the inverse, being the subliminal area of consciousness or the soul's nether part which harbours the murky, mindless, and passive alluvium of the psyche, and which has to be totally dominated if there is to be any spiritual progress at all. Hypnotism does indeed function in just this area, which is a good reason why spiritual masters eschew it, the other obvious reason being that it leads to nowhere.

Not that the Seigneur of the Prieuré failed to stress the necessity for an active attitude accompanied with intensive effort and self-inflicted suffering: the cult of the disagreeable had the status of a dogma; flux and ceaseless change were in the permanent scheme of things, *serenity* being a word not found in his vocabulary. 'The greater the efforts that are made,' he said, 'the greater the new demands.'

Again: 'Ordinary efforts do not count. *Only super-efforts count.*' And since he taught that 'there is only "self-initiation",' no one will dispute that a Draconian effort must be required on the part of a volitionless 'machine' to accomplish this incredible feat, which is—as his inimitable Mullah Nassr Eddin would say—'to hoist oneself over the moon by one's bootstraps.'

What actually took place is demonstrated in the cases of Peters and Bennett above: when a man through toil, suffering, or sickness had reached the limit of his endurance, and his habitual vital resistance—i.e., the legacy of his 'Kundabuffer'—was low, the moment was propitious for the transmission of *hanbledzoin* into the 'psychic bloodstream'—which is an inversion of the spiritual way, where the disciple who has faithfully and integrally followed his master's teachings to the limit of his capacities is reduced to a state of worldly impoverishment favoring an influx of Divine Grace.

De Hartmann notwithstanding insisted that the operative power was 'magnetic' rather than 'hypnotic', 'because all Mr Gurdjieff's Teaching leads men toward being free of suggestion.' This point merits examination. Gurdjieff considered himself the possessor of what he called *Zvarnoharno*, something Bennett translates as 'aura of kingship', going on to say that it was this quality which among other things obliged the man to feign 'outrageous behavior' as a means of thwarting incipient idol-worship.

> There is no question [says Peters], that Gurdjieff had an unbe-lievable (unless you've seen it) *awareness* of other people. It was nothing so limited as mind-reading or thought-transference. He seemed to know so much about the human processes . . . that he was conscious of everything that took place within any human being he happened to observe. . . . I have never known him to be wrong. . . . It was difficult to resist such obvious learning or 'power' and, in fact, there was no reason to resist it. Contrary to the reports about him, there was no evidence that he did any-thing to anyone that could be considered 'evil'.[2]

Leaving this last remark for the moment in parentheses, we can now let Gurdjieff tell it his own way, with the aviso that 'any human being he happened to observe' covers only those whom destiny brought under his scrutiny and cannot *de facto* be expanded to encompass the overwhelming majority of his contemporaries, of whom most—including many of the foremost—have never even heard his name, not to mention all those with spiritual and intellec-tual dimensions inaccessible to his observational techniques:

> I know what is state of each man around me because I am edu-cated man, I have knowledge. You must always try have consider-ateness for state of surrounding if you wish be objective *bon-ton*. . . . You notice never anyone take offence anything I say?—

---

2. He loved little children, after all, teaching them always to honor and obey their parents; and he made a *Père Noël formidable* at his rollicking Christmas par-ties.

never man angry with me when *I* tell? You know why? Because I
tell exact how is, objective truth.

This incontestable magnetism, which Gurdjieff bequeathed to pos-
terity, was even presumed by him to reverberate backwards in time.
Thus, when in preparing a pit in a cellar at the Prieuré for the winter
storage of carrots he dug through some lime, sand, and straw and
came upon a 'super-most-super-heavenly-nectar,' namely, twenty-
seven bottles of old Calvados, it was immediately clear to him that
this 'divine liquid' had been left there as a libation by the monks of
yore, whose 'intuitive perspicacity . . . thanks to their pious lives'
allowed them to precognize the advent of an Eminence able to
appreciate and propagate their 'ideals' 'to the next generation';
which said libation the predestined beneficiary forthright consumed—along with some two hundred bottles of 'no less sublime
old Armagnac to top off 'this totality of cosmic substances.'
    So much for magnetism. Back now to de Hartmann's idea that
the Gurdjieffian way leads towards freedom from suggestion: John
Middleton Murry did not believe this, and he had been forced to
investigate the Fontainebleau Institute closely, given his wife's
involvement. An editorial note at the conclusion of *Katherine Mansfield's Letters to John Middleton Murry 1913–1922*, which he published, manifests enough neutrality and magnanimity in its
assessment of the circumstances culminating in her death to permit
serious reflection on some remarks of his written to the *London
Daily News* several months after she died. He observed in effect that
the Institute did not resolve the problem that it claimed to resolve.
Instead, it simply plunged its members for the time being into a sort
of unconsciousness. It was as though they had been given some
kind of drug, a very efficacious and very penetrating drug, but who
could say if in the end any benefit was produced, any really positive
result?
    However unbiased this opinion may be, it is admittedly still from
the outside; but there are other witnesses from the inside: Pierre
Minet, for example, co-founder along with René Daumal and other
French literati of the somewhat surrealistic poetry movement, *Le
Grand Jeu*, who was briefly brought into Gurdjieffianism by Daumal, himself known for the allegorical account of his experiences,

therein entitled *Le Mont Analogue*. Here are some extracts from Minet's autobiographical work, *La Défaite*:

'Begin by letting this idea sink in that you are nothing, no, not even a grain of sand in the desert, absolutely nothing, the naught.' This beat all philosophies, this affirmation. It transported me with rapture. It opened up infinite horizons. At first, how much more agreeable it was to be nothing instead of this mass of pitiful, sad and boring corpuscles that had to be called something. Absolute negation, how restful! Not a thought, not a feeling could resist it. . . .
This did not last for long. 'You are nothing. You can be, everything. You can be. Only watch out, to right, to left, attention; more attention, always attention, don't identify yourself with your sensations, you are like a baby learning to walk! Not so fast! Follow your governess!' The governess, that was me: me also. Both the brat and the nanny. How could one avoid being mistaken? Nevertheless I did my utmost to play these roles correctly.[3]

Minet says his whole life revolved around the three hours weekly of lectures:

We sat down, no cigarettes please, one more little victory over yourselves, small streams make big rivers! A dozen persons, then, sagely seated, to hear excellent metaphysical recipes. Very sensible, all this; undeniable the consciousness that is unaware of itself, the mechanical man, and even man number 1, man number 2, man number 3, man number 4, whom you will be, the day when hens get teeth. But the more one advanced, the more this became theoretical, to believe that we were not made of flesh and bones and that we could depend entirely on these graphs, these figures, these circles which claimed to explain everything, to resolve everything, and which led straight to immortality. Cosmic laws, the influence of planets on my behavior, the moon as chaperon, no, I didn't recognize myself any more. This no longer interested me. I groused. I now had the impression of

---

3. Minet gives an eloquent testimony here to the trials of 'self-initiation'.

participating in a juggling act. Thus, one and all we only began to exist after having thrown overboard what best characterized us. Our tastes, our most tenacious sufferings, our fondest attachments, into the sea! Really, it was asking a lot. Too much. And all this in order to gain peace, the virgin awe of the catechumen. . . . Finally, I broke off. I refused to let myself be robbed any longer. And I gained back my muck. To be sure, it did not smell good. But stench for stench, I still preferred mine to that of the newborn babe!

Reflections along a similar vein determined another French writer, the journalist and editor Paul Sérant, to quit the movement:

I was no doubt less affected by the outward world; conversely the exclusive attention on myself ended by creating in me an unbearable sensation of disgust. I had aspired to be liberated from the world; I now aspired to be liberated from myself. Instead of feeling released from my 'mechanical' chains, I had impression of forging new ones, infinitely heavier in that they abolished the spontaneity of the instincts and feelings, spontaneity which could render so light at times the constraint of being nothing but a machine! Maybe I was no longer a machine, but not to be one any more, what a dreadful nostalgia! This consciousness which I had supposed would shatter my limitations had instead only procured for me the most terrible of tyrannies. . . .[4] The more I plunged into myself, the less did I discover this 'greater than I'! The 'I' which I encompassed only infected me more and more

---

4. These words recall a cry of distress coming from another place and time, but decidedly analogous in content:

Somehow they (the 'Berlin Brotherhood') all seemed to me to be men without souls. They were desperate, determined seekers into realms of being with which earth had no sympathy, and which in consequence abstracted them from all human feelings or human emotions. . . . In their companionship I felt abandoned of my kind. . . . If the knowledge I had purchased was indeed a reality, there were times when I deemed it was neither good nor lawful for man to possess it. I often envied the peaceful unconsciousness of the outer world, and would gladly have gone back to the simple faith of my childhood, and then have closed my eyes in eternal sleep sooner than awaken to the terrible unrest which had possessed me since I had crossed the safe boundaries of the visible, and entered upon the illimitable wastes of the invisible' (*Ghost Land; or Researches into the Mysteries of Occultism*, anonymous, tr. and ed. by Emma Hardinge Britten, Boston, 1876, pp 47–48).

with a frightful nausea. [For Sérant] there is no true spirituality without worship. Ascesis, renouncement, detachment, and the void only have a meaning when ordained by Love. That this Love is not to be confused with the more immediate aspects of the sentiments is perfectly clear to me, and such moreover is the attitude of the great mystics. But it is essential not to destroy in the soul the very possibility for worship.

Sérant observed that his erstwhile companions trampled blithely on morality, culture, civilization, religion, sneering when one spoke about scruples of conscience: 'The really extraordinary feature,' says Bennett, 'is that the way to liberation is not by virtuous living, but by fulfilling the obligation to transform energies needed for the Cosmic Purpose.'

I noticed [writes Sérant] that the effort of consciousness had created among these people a rather suspicious mixture of pretension, selfishness, and pride (or more exactly, self-satisfaction).[5] These faults are naturally the lot of all mortals, but what seemed to me grave here is that they were methodically cultivated in the name of non-identification, lucidity, and self-awareness. Obviously when it is taken for granted that all men are machines while one is oneself emerging from this category, the risk of a dangerous temptation arises: if other people are machines, why not use them as such? Duplicity then becomes a very legitimate form of training in sharper self-awareness.

This idea is echoed in a remark Madame de Salzmann made to René Guénon whom she sought out in Cairo shortly after her master's death with hope of getting counsel (*Vous voilà dans de beaux draps*). 'Gurdjieff,' she told the French metaphysician, 'rarely spoke the truth'—an admission which goes at any rate to show that Gurdjieff practiced what he preached, one of his dicta being, 'Truth can only come to people *in the form of a lie.*'

---

5. In a lecture at Fontainebleau recorded by Bennett, Gurdjieff, taught with supreme syllogism:

Pride of Self is the sign of being in possession of oneself. . . . Pride of Self is 'I'. 'I' is God. Consequently it is needful to have pride.

But when this attitude is adopted, one may insensibly—thanks to the soporific effects of hypnosis—transgress the fragile demarcation line separating the practice of contradiction from the spirit of perversity:

> This is where a sort of spiritual inversion occurs [continues Sérant], infinitely more perilous than *immoralism accepted as such*.... The real spiritual danger begins the moment when Good is called Evil, and Evil Good. The perversion thus created is well-nigh irremediable.

This point is brought home by Charles Duits, cited in Michel Waldberg's recent French book, *Gurdjieff*.

> Beelzebub, an old man filled with goodness [he assures us], whose action has clearly been nothing short of 'angelic', is taken by human beings for the devil in person. Thus, right from the start we have a key at our disposal: men see the world upside down, such is their affliction; they take Angels for Devils, and *vice versa*.

While Bennett does not quite have that to say about Beelzebub, he argues lamely that this personage 'was a minor member of the Chaldaean Pantheon . . . rather than . . . a synonym for Satan'—a particularly weak argument when Gurdjieff himself has given the secret away with his explanation in *The Herald of Coming Good* that he chose for 'principal hero' someone 'as a likely witness' to the appearance 'of the first human beings on earth.' Now apart from God, who else was 'witness' to the proceedings in the Garden except the serpent?

All this, of course, is so much poppycock to Gurdjieff, who announces,

> I have set myself under essence-oath . . . to prove, without fail . . . to all my contemporaries, the absurdity of all their inherent ideas concerning the suppositious existences [*sic*] of a certain 'other world' with its famous and so beautiful 'paradise' and its so repugnant a 'hell'.

Theological 'wiseacring' about Good and Evil, future reward and future punishment, has no place in his world view. But the denial of immediate and by consequence ultimate Good and Evil does not of itself suffice to banish these concepts, nor does it guarantee immunity from mistaking the one for the other—assuming the concepts exist, as his exposition in the following paragraph allows us to believe they do.

Not forgetting Peters' remark on 'evil' that was left in parentheses, we can let Gurdjieff answer this himself with a saying from 'very ancient times' to the effect that

> every stick always has two ends ... one of which [he goes on to observe], is considered good and the other bad. ... Briefly, if I exercise my privilege and take the good end of the stick, then the bad end must inevitably fall 'on the reader's head.'

Or, as he has his Mulla Nassr Eddin say:

> For our sins, God has sent us two kind of physicians, one kind to help us die, and the other to prevent us living.

Call it then magnetism, hypnotism, or what you like, and accept Gurdjieff's beguiling (because no commitment is asked) disclaimer of initiation ('There is not, nor can there be, an outward initiation'), the fact remains that he transmitted very real powers, as the instrument of 'agencies' to which Bennett gives the name 'Demiurgic Intelligences'. During all his years of teaching Ouspensky remained convinced that the Gurdjieffian 'System' emanated from a 'Great Source'.

> But there is no chance for us to find it by looking. ... It is much better hidden than people suppose. Therefore, our only hope is that the Source will seek us out. That is why I am giving these lectures in London. If those who have the real knowledge see that we can be useful to them, they may send someone.

What he did not know was that he was already being very useful to 'them', but that they could not co-operate any more than they were already doing, being in Bennett's words, 'agencies that we cannot perceive with our senses or even know with our minds.'

This 'something' moreover that was transmitted does not—to repeat—easily wash off, even with those who have attempted purgation. 'You poisoned for life,' we have seen Gurdjieff tell Peters, who himself confesses that 'even in death, he continued to have an enormous and troubling influence over me.' We likewise saw how Pauwels remained saddled with 'the ambiguities of the profoundest respect,' which finds a resonance in Sérant's declaration that

> it is not at all my intention to condemn the Teaching outright. I remain persuaded that it conveys elements which an authentic spiritual search cannot afford to neglect; ... in a word, I liked and continue to like the aristocratic, even Nietzschean, aspect of the Teaching.[6]

This last remark is frankly misplaced. Certainly the spiritual elect constitutes a great aristocracy, even including its more 'outlandish' manifestations—the 'Fools in Christ' of Hesychasm, for example, or the *Malāmatīyah* ('People of Blame') in Islam, the 'Immortals' in Taoism, or the *Heyokas* of the Sioux Indians—which always derive from suprahuman and not subhuman factors; certainly moreover the Gurdjieffian movement has always attracted aristocrats aplenty.[7] But if one has to search for a word to describe it, then snobbism—and not aristocracy—best catches the prevailing tone—this 'attitude of almost beatific secrecy' already mentioned by Peters, who observed that Gurdjieff's

---

6. Pauwels cites from an article in the September 1927 issue of the review *New Adelphi* by a Dr Young, for twenty years an English surgeon and later psychiatrist and disciple of Jung, who spent a year at the Prieuré. With a cold medical eye he reached the studied conviction that whatever the appearances, Gurdjieff's real motivation was the obscure and Luciferian quest for powers (*siddhis*) as taught through brutal methods in certain Mongolian monasteries where he probably received initiation—powers acquired with a view to ruling our planet. 'However,' concludes Dr Young, 'I would not want it thought that this experience for me resulted in the loss pure and simple of a year of my time. Far from that, I am convinced that I greatly profited from what is of value in this teaching.'

7. The collaboration of aristocrats in a movement is not *ipso facto* a guarantee of canonicity. The Freemasonic conflagration sweeping through eighteenth-century Europe was fuelled by aristocracy, Rasputin played to the Russian Court, and certainly aristocrats participated in Hitler's rise to power.

students, with contented, superior smiles on their faces would declare publicly that they had at last found the 'real thing', or a 'great teaching', etc., etc., and then, upon being challenged, seemed unable to explain what it was, or how it worked.

The grossness of approach (starting with 'men are machines'), the studied insolence (as in the 'idiots' toast'), and Gurdjieff's predilection 'to wiseacre full blast' ill accord with what most people understand by aristocracy—a rank furthermore which he hated, calling aristocrats 'jokes of nature' and 'misconceptions' whose ability to exist on our planet puzzled 'even the great cunning Lucifer' to the point where 'he grew so intensely thoughtful that all the hairs of the tip of his tail turned quite gray.' Gurdjieff by the way would roar with laughter when such passages from *Beelzebub* were read aloud to him.

But aristocratic elements aside, Sérant's message is clear. Pauwels attempts to explain the grip of Gurdjieffianism—this 'subterranean and darkly fascinating world'—with a description from the African jungle of how hunters trap monkeys. They attach a hollow gourd to a coconut palm, toss in some peanuts, and disappear. The monkey soon swings down from the tree and reaches his hand through the narrow neck to seize a fistful of nuts. But now he is unable to extricate the swollen hand, and the frightened beast clenching his booty ever more tightly falls prey to his captors.

> I have often thought of this fruit when trying to disengage myself from the teaching of Gurdjieff.... But it was very difficult and I was like most members of these groups: prisoner of my own ambition, henceforth doomed to desiccation, and, like the monkey, fated for the cage or death.

Peters and other writers repeatedly comment on Gurdjieff's lusty humor, so conspicuously lacking in his disciples, and it is true that photographs of them typically betray a certain torpor, a sadness or melancholy and vacancy of expression. Yet it seems obvious enough that if Gurdjieff had reason for indulging in laughter, by the same token his disciples had reason to refrain.

✪

Gurdjieff made some telling observations on another subject:

> Black magic does not in any way mean magic of evil. . . . No one
> ever does anything for the sake of evil, in the interests of evil.
> Everyone always does everything in the interests of good *as he
> understands it.* . . . Black magic may be quite altruistic, may strive
> after the good of humanity. . . . But what can be called black
> magic has always one definite characteristic. This characteristic is
> the tendency to use people for some, even the best of aims, *with-
> out their knowledge and understanding*, either by producing in
> them faith and infatuation or by acting upon them through fear.
> But it must be remembered in this connection that a 'black magi-
> cian', whether good or evil [*sic*], has at all events been at a school.
> He has learned something, has heard something, knows some-
> thing. He is simply a 'half-educated man' who has either been
> turned out of a school or who has himself left a school having
> decided that he already knows enough, that he does not want to
> be in subordination any longer, and that he can work indepen-
> dently and even direct the work of others. All 'work' of this kind
> can produce only subjective results, that is to say, it can only
> increase deception and increase sleep instead of decreasing them.
> Nevertheless something can be learned from a 'black magician'
> although in the wrong way. He can sometimes by accident even
> tell the truth.

To whom was the speaker of these lines holding up a mirror?

Aleister Crowley, the notorious English magician, once paid Gurdjieff an apparently unsolicited visit at Fontainebleau. The 'Forest
Philosophers' gathered round in anticipation of what would even-
tuate, the visiting mage having challenged the resident one to a dis-
play in magic, but it came to a disappointing draw, Gurdjieff,
declining to expose certain powers which he nonetheless claimed to
possess. Crowley for his part refused to stage a solo performance,
and he left convinced, according to Peters, that his rival was either 'a
fake,' or else 'an inferior black magician.'

This episode can be interpreted in several ways. First, it is common knowledge that magicians do not lose any love on one another, each being jealous of his demesne. Secondly, Crowley was ostentatiously a 'bounder' and master showman, whereas Gurdjieff, passed for a 'serious' man with a concern for society, being a 'scientific philosopher', *maestro* of 'sacred dance', and herald of a new path for humanity based on the hoariest of forgotten wisdoms. It must also be remembered that the resolve he formulated never to exploit his *hanbledzoin* for self-seeking ends left him literally 'indifferent' to the effect he created on people—thoroughly confident that his resolve would make the necessary effect felt without the need to implicate himself 'egotistically' in any contrived 'theatrics'. Transposed into spiritual terms, this would be the equivalent of sacrificing one's personal gifts for the Glory of God. Gurdjieff, in other words, was a 'dedicated' man, working for a cause larger than himself. Thirdly, Crowley was the High Initiate of Freemasonry and so many of the occultisms and secret societies which Gurdjieff openly professed to scorn, saying that 'their work simply consists in aping'—which whatever the case certainly enhanced the credibility of his own method by opposing it to the pseudo-initiations and pseudo-esoteric systems that are conventionally considered to be false; Crowley by contrast from his viewpoint might well regard the other thaumaturge as a kind of 'freak intruder' from Turkestan, answering to none of the more 'orthodox' cabalisms. Fourthly, there is just the possibility that the two men had some business in common that escaped the notice of the others present—a 'mandate' from the Order of Thule, for example, since Gurdjieff despite his barbs at occultism always claimed to be in contact with a 'Hidden Center'; but this is to speculate in the dark.

❂

Another teaching Gurdjieff honored with all the *noblesse oblige* its conviction entailed went to the effect, on Denis Saurat's testimony, that women could scarcely hope to come by souls except through sexual contact and union with a man. Thus, to hear Bennett tell it, he recompensed brief spells of austerity with 'unbridled periods' of venery:

> At times, he had sexual relations not only with almost any woman who happened to come within the sphere of his influence, but also with his own pupils. Quite a number of his women pupils bore him children.

The idea was bruited about that 'only those women who had slept with him were really initiated into his Work.' And yet in fact there were some women disciples who had no relationship of this kind with him at all; and it would sometimes even happen that a young lady upon receiving a hint to knock on his door and going in the expectation of a remarkable spiritual adventure would discover him apparently astonished to find her there and would be rebuffed with a bag of sweets as a solace, whereas those who went with no illusions got their relationship and perchance some instruction too. For

> he was very insistent that sex should be separated from the intellectual and emotional life of man. Sex was sex and, if treated as such, was not only a legitimate but even a necessary part of the process of our development.

With most people, however, he said 'it is the principal motive force of all mechanicalness,' and to the average man woman is no more than a 'handkerchief'. 'Do you think people go to the theatre or to church to pray or to see some new play?' he asked Ouspensky. 'That is only for the sake of appearances. The principle thing, in the theatre as well as in church, is that there will be a lot of women or a lot of men. This is the center of gravity of all gatherings.' Gurdjieff, once—in 1933—treated Peters to a demonstration of this at the former's New York apartment in the Henry Hudson Hotel, where Peters was convoked. When he arrived he was asked to wash dishes and prepare vegetables for 'some very important people' who were coming to dinner. Gurdjieff said he needed Peters to give him an 'English lesson' consisting of words for all those parts and functions of the body 'that were not in the dictionary.' By the time Gurdjieff had mastered the four-letter words and obscene phrases the guests started arriving, who turned out to be some fifteen 'well-dressed, well-mannered New Yorkers,' of which a number were reporters or journalists.

After staging a late and obsequious entry, the host humbly began responding at table to the guests' blasé questions on his work and reasons for visiting America, when with a wink to his 'English teacher' he suddenly changed tone and explained that the sad degeneration of humankind and its transformation into a substance only describable by a four-letter expletive was particularly striking in their country, whence his coming to observe this phenomenon in the raw. The cause behind this distressing state of affairs, he continued, lay in the fact that people—especially Americans—never followed the dictates of intelligence or propriety, but only that of their genital organs. Then, signalling out one particularly handsome woman, he complimented her on her attire and make-up, after which he confided that in all honesty between them the real explanation behind her adornment was an irresistible sexual urge she felt for some particular person—graphically spelled out by Gurdjieff, with his newly-acquired vocabulary. Before the guests could react he launched into a discourse on his own sexual prowess, followed by intimate and detailed descriptions of the sexual mores of various races and nations.

By the time the dinner was over and the guests well plied with 'good old Armagnac as always,' they lost their inhibitions and joined in an exchange of obscenities which soon became more than verbal. Gurdjieff, retired with the lady whom he had insulted, and the others, by now conditioned to believe that an orgy or something was in the tenor of the evening, began entangling physically in different rooms of the apartment in various stages of undress.

Just when the carousel was at a climax Gurdjieff, briskly disengaged himself and thundered forth orders for the revels to cease, proclaiming that the lesson had been accomplished, that the guests had already amply verified through their comportment the soundness of his observations made earlier in the evening—that thanks to him they were now partly conscious of their true condition, and that he would gladly accept from them cheques and cash in payment for this 'important lesson.' Peters noted—without surprise, knowing Gurdjieff—that the take came to '*several thousand dollars.*'

When everyone had left, Gurdjieff went into the kitchen to help Peters with the dishes, asking at the same time how he had enjoyed the evening.

'I was disgusted,' came the reply. Gurdjieff laughed and scrutinized his companion with a 'piercing look'. 'Is fine feeling you have—this disgust. But now is necessary ask yourself one question. With who you disgusted?'

❂

One thing that 'appalled' Peters among both the admirers and detractors[8] of Gurdjieff was the emotional, personal, or vindictive— as the case might be—reactions to his person and method. Rarely did anyone evaluate him with objective detachment. Even his proponents would sometimes manifest disgust at what they considered to be his 'dirty' or 'insanitary' habits. Peters was the first to know about this, having cleaned the maestro's room for two years at the Prieuré. But he argues rather weakly against the repeated contention 'that a great teacher is, of necessity, clean,' reasoning:

This seems to me to be the equivalent of accepting Christianity after an investigation of the bathing habits of Jesus Christ. Or is 'cleanliness next to Godliness' after all? And does that old saw actually refer to physical cleanliness?

Well, it certainly in no way excludes it, and the best response here is from the *Discourses* of Epictetus, the chapter 'On Cleanliness' (IV. XI, translated by P.E. Matheson):

Since the gods are by nature pure and unalloyed, just insofar as men have approached them by virtue of reason, they have a tendency to purity and cleanliness. But since it is impossible for

8. For Peters these detractors were of two kinds: vituperative ex-students, and scholars who considered themselves critics 'of any teaching that touched on the occult' and who 'seem to me to pounce on [Gurdjieff] because he did not live up to their conception of orthodoxy.' But this last remark is tantamount to saying that orthodoxy is by definition subjective and by nature purely psychological; with a facile phrase objective criteria are thus condemned to the dustheap.

their nature to be entirely pure, being composed of such stuff as it is, the reason which they have received endeavours, so far as in it lies, to make this stuff clean.

The primary and fundamental purity is that of the soul, and so with impurity. The soul's impurity consists in bad judgements, and purification consists in producing in it right judgements. . . . And one ought to endeavour, as far as may be, to achieve a similar cleanliness in one's body too. . . . It was impossible for men's feet not to be made muddy and dirty when they pass through mud and dirt; for this reason nature provided water and hands to wash with. . . .

But who does not turn from a man who is dirty, odorous, foul-complexioned, more than from one who is bespattered with muck? The smell of the latter is external and accidental, that of the former comes from want of tendance; it is from within, and shows a sort of inward rottenness.

'But Socrates rarely washed.'

Why, his body was clean and bright, nay, it was so gracious and agreeable... he might have never washed or bathed, if he had liked: I tell you his ablutions, if rare, were powerful. . . .

By the gods, when the young man feels the first stirrings of philosophy I would rather he came to me with his hair sleek than dishevelled and dirty: for that shows a sort of reflection of the beautiful, and a longing for the comely, and where he imagines these to be, there he spends his effort. . . .

Here is a young man worthy to be loved, here is an old man worthy to love and to be loved, one to whom a man is to hand over his son to be instructed: daughters and young men will come to him, if it so chance, and for what? That he may discourse to them on a dunghill? God forbid. All eccentricity springs from some human source, but this comes near to being inhuman altogether.

Frithjof Schuon has shown[9] how certain voluntaristic and sentimental excesses in the Christian sphere since the time of the Renaissance have made it possible to equate intelligence with pride, which

9. See for example 'Paradoxes de l'expression spirituelle en Islam et ailleurs', *Revue Philosophique*, January–March, 1974.

in itself is comprehensible, but which leads to other equations, like beauty with sin—hence ugliness with virtue, or again, cleanliness with sin—hence dirtiness with virtue. This does not mean that Gurdjieff's disciples—all presumably of Christian origin—adhered to any particular pietistic persuasions, although some belonged to the Orthodox Church; but it does mean that the prevalence of such currents in Christianity has left its tendencies and traces—albeit unconsciously—even on those who have abandoned their faith.

It is not known that Gurdjieff, despite his years in Islamic countries, had any Muslims for disciples; and other considerations apart, the stress in Islam on intelligence, beauty, and purity would make it unthinkable for a Muslim still conscious of his heritage to be drawn into Gurdjieff's world.

❂

Certain facets of the personality sponsoring Harmonious Development are revealed in his travelling manners. He was perfectly capable, for example, of detaining the midnight sleeper from New York to Chicago ten minutes' overtime by somehow convincing an official on the platform at Grand Central Station that he was an eminent personage having urgent business to conclude with the delegation of votaries thronging about; when finally shoved on board an already moving train followed by a traveling companion—in this case Peters—and some seven pieces of luggage loaded with books, medicine, clothing, food, and liquor—of noisily complaining about the interruption, and ordering a bed prepared immediately. Appalled at learning that his berth was thirteen cars ahead—of sitting on a suitcase to light a cigarette and groaning loudly when told that smoking was prohibited except in the men's room (berths on American sleeping cars at that period were partitioned solely from the corridor by curtains); of awakening nearly all passengers (most having boarded early) during the forty-five-minute trek through the train with complaints about the rude handling he was undergoing, and when finally reaching his berth, of unpacking his bags in search of food and liquor until forced by Peters into the men's quarters, there to start a loud discourse on the terrible service and shoddy way in which he—a very important man—was being treated, yet when warned by the conductor and the porter that he courted the risk of expulsion at the next station, of staring around in wide-eyed innocence; of at last going to bed all the while lamenting loudly about his thirst and need for cigarettes and so forth until more menaces from the porter finally decided him to sleep; of raising a rumpus in the dining car the next morning—which he finally reached after an hour's dressing with repeated walks down the aisle in his underwear—on finding no yoghurts or other (then) exotic foods so necessary for his highly specialized digestive processes, vividly detailed to the waiter and head steward, whereupon he consumed amidst grumbles a hearty American breakfast; of passing the remainder of the journey in his Pullman car, smoking incessantly despite passengers' complaints and threats from the porter, drinking heavily, and intermittently producing foods—mainly evil-smelling cheeses—all the time apologizing profusely to the irate passengers even while inventing new ways to annoy and offend. And when at last reaching the group awaiting him on the platform at Chicago, of telling them all about what a ghastly trip he had had, and laying the entire responsibility for it on the already mortified Peters.

Are we to suppose, by the way, that all this was a comedy staged by the possessor of *Zvarnoharno* in view of protecting the passengers, conductor, and porter from incipient idol worship, or to test their mettle as potential disciples? A devotee would no doubt reply that a King can do as he pleases—such runs the reasoning of the world.

Bennett went through a similar ordeal in putting Gurdjieff on board a boat at Le Havre in 1948. When his charge, who had insisted on a single cabin, found there were none on the outside, he announced that he would leave the ship at Southampton, ordering Bennett to arrange to meet him there the next morning. Then he stormed off to the deserted grill-room, telling his companion to fetch the basket from Paris that had 'bottles of Armagnac, jars of caviare and zakuskas of various kinds.' This of course, infuriated the stewards, 'but he mollified them with a generous tip.' Bennett himself was only able to mollify Gurdjieff by proposing toast after toast as 'Director of toasts,' drinking with him until the ship left at midnight.

❖

Some readers who have held on thus far may by now be wondering just what Gurdjieff had for all his magnetism that could induce discerning men and women to submit their spiritual development into his safekeeping.

It has been seen how people could scarcely maintain a neutral attitude when confronted with this person: one either reacted with a strong aversion, or else one was irresistibly drawn into his orbit with something approaching total commitment—not to mention those cases where an initial repulsion turned later into utter rapture. The fact that it is likewise a peculiarity of evil either to fascinate or repel, while it cannot necessarily be adduced as an *ad rem* proof of anything, must at least be weighed into consideration by the serious reader along with everything else.

Gurdjieff came to a West of scattered values with a cynical eye that saw clearly—almost—the trash that is modern civilization, the mess that is modern man. This in itself is a positive 'contribution'. But his vision was negative and destructive—hence the ambiguity recognized by Pauwels. For if he was keenly aware of man's foibles, he suffered a corresponding blindness to man's virtues. *Beelzebub* on the surface thus appears as a heavy-handed sneer at the human race, while on a deeper level it really reveals Gurdjieff's own obsession with modalities of consciousness depassing his competence. He identified himself unequivocally with the 'Devil', only, having this identification, he naturally did not envisage the 'Devil' as 'evil', but simply as 'realistic'. And yet if something of this became ontologically too transparent in his writings, he would recast the passage in order to 'bury the dog deeper,' as he put it.[10] He even repudiated *The Herald of Coming Good* and had it withdrawn from circulation.

10. Bennett attempts to side-step this expression with the argument that 'the dog is Sirius the dog star, which stands for the spirit of wisdom in the Zoroastrian tradition.' But he comes much nearer the heart of the matter when he adds that Gurdjieff did not wish 'to be analyzed and criticized by philosophers and theologians, so he wrote in language that learned beings would not trouble to read.'

The point here is that the emergence of Gurdjieff, coincided with the moment when reflective Western intellectuals were having their first second-thoughts about Progress, and he brought, to begin with, an explanation for the existent state of affairs, and secondly, an 'ancient' remedy pried out of the East purporting to get man back once again onto the right track.

Was he then, or not, an evolutionist? True to his contradictory character, the answer is: both yes and no. The World process, he taught, is concurrently evolutionary and involutionary, being based on 'the great fundamental cosmic law Trogoautoegocrat,' namely, the 'reciprocal-maintenance-of-every-thing-that-exists,' which without elaborating the scheme comes down to a sort of 'galactic ecology' where man, assisted by various Demiurges and Higher Intelligences patterned somewhat along Gnostic and Manichaean lines, shares with God—'OUR COMMON FATHER OMNI-BEING END-LESSNESS,' or whatever—responsibility for running the cosmic show. *Reciprocal*, because it suffices an error in judgement on the part of either God (who it will be remembered is not omnipotent) or man to put the Universe out of joint. God set to rights an earlier miscalculation of his by removing from man the pernicious organ Kundabuffer, and it is now for man to cease basking in the dreams which are this organ's after effects, and, combining the 'wisdom' of the East with the 'energy' of the West, to breach his subconscious-ness and thus break loose from the tyranny of modern technology and all the cosmically disruptive idiocies invented by three-brained scientists bent—as the esteemed Mullah Nassr Eddin sagely said—on 'making a gnat swallow an elephant'—before they smash the world to smithereens with a blast, once more in the sage's words—'like a Jericho-trumpet-in-crescendo.'[11] Gurdjieff chided Peters at their last meeting:

11. It is curious that Beelzebub's own solution for mankind's woes is to have planted into men a new organ in place of the former Kundabuffer, that would render every 'three-brained being' perpetually 'cognizant of the inevitability of his own death as well as of the death of everyone upon whom his eyes or attention rests.' While traditionally the remembrance of death is also enjoined on us, it is for a reason that is well expressed, for example, in *The Imitation of Christ*: 'Learn now to die to the world, that thou mayest then begin to live with Christ.'

Americans drop bomb on Japan, yes? What you think of your America now?

By the Law of Reciprocal Maintenance, all energy, matter, and life patterns or 'essence classes' to be found in the Universe maintain and sustain one another through a delicately equilibrated evolving/involuting cosmic cannibalism (it will be remembered that the moon fattens on the earth, and *vice versa*).

One might wonder how this galactic ecological system can be reconciled with '*a way against nature, against God*'; but the incompatibility between the two conceptions does not seem to ruffle some people, who apparently find it flattering to enter upon a partnership with the 'Higher Hosts' in a work of Reciprocal Maintenance aimed at keeping the World on an even keel, that would free our planet of 'hate, madness and war,' in Margaret Anderson's words.

Yet if these Western intellectuals looked to the core of the matter, they would see that the rituals in all religions are for maintaining an equilibrium between Heaven and Earth—by symbolism, analogy, and sympathetic correspondence. 'Thy will be done in earth, as it is in heaven' is the basis for it in Christianity. Islam (submission to the Divine Will) proclaims that man is Viceregent on Earth (*khalīfa fi'l-arḍ*), and responsible to God for the right ordering of everything. *Dharmashāstra* enjoins on Hindus what is necessary here. The Far East teaches that man is Mediator between Heaven and Earth, and the American Indians possessed one of the most perfectly functioning 'ecological systems' the world has ever known, until destroyed by 'three-brained' Europeans gone astray from their own heritage.

Moreover, since every religion in its mode teaches that man is in a state of disequilibrium, illusion, ignorance, fall, or rebellion, why do some people only prick up their ears when Gurdjieff says it?

The origin and cause of thoughts lies in the splitting up, by man's transgression, of his single and simple memory, which has thus lost the memory of God and, becoming multiple instead of simple, and varied instead of single, has fallen a prey to its own forces,' writes St Gregory of Sinai.

Or as Plato puts it: 'The soul . . . by reason of lust had become the principle accomplice in her own captivity.'

This finds its echo in John Smith the Platonist: 'Those turbulent and unruly, uncertain and unconstant motions of passion and self-will that dwell in degenerate minds, divide them perpetually from themselves, and are always moulding several factions and tumultuous combinations within them against the dominion of reason.'

But now comes Gurdjieff with a startling new formula. MAN IS A MACHINE: Here is the stuff that strikes a chord in modern minds, proclaimed to boot by a 'scientific philosopher' who is a forthright materialist and sceptic—hence a 'realist'. And a way based on 'sciences' of the highest antiquity lost to everybody but himself is proposed for resolving the dilemma straight at the core without having to have recourse to all the clutter of a religion. What if for the unremitting pains one takes, Harmonious Development proves in practice to be but the metamorphosis into a high-precision robot? Well, 'the game is worth the candle,' and this is presumably better at least than remaining—say—just a broken-down gramophone. Anyhow, the Institute with its ramifications has always been particularly attractive to artists, writers, musicians, and professional people in general, namely, those of a high sensitivity with an equally high ego-content—people worldly and complicated yet idealistic, strong yet vulnerable, with the innate human desire to dominate and transcend the tragedies of the undisciplined ego.

Still, how can human beings of such sensitivity stomach the grossness prevalent throughout? For one thing, the dances and the music and the complicated doctrines lend an aura of 'dignity' to the movement; for another, the thaumaturge's proneness to shock with outrageous behavior is often compared to the techniques employed by Zen *roshis* to precipitate *Satori*. Only, here the analogy does not hold, since Zen—where vulgarity to begin with is totally absent—functions within the framework and protection of Buddhism, of which it is a particular extension. The *roshi*, acting under inspiration in a revealed and living tradition, is applying procedures of proven efficacity to qualified disciples finely attuned by strict monastic disciplines to receive them.

It must be recognized, however, that Gurdjieff offered in a 'complete' way a very beguiling show of cold unsentimental inquiry regarding his investigations into 'the miraculous', combined with

great practicality and earthy common sense—with a shrewdness at
times almost passing for wisdom.

Take for example what he says on Eastern music after having
explained about quarter tones, and even 'a seventh of a tone':

To foreigners, Eastern music seems monotonous, they only wonder at its crudity and musical poverty. But what sounds like one
note to them is a whole melody for the local inhabitants—a melody contained in one note. This kind of melody is much more
difficult than ours. If an Eastern musician makes a mistake in his
melody the result is cacophony for them, but for a European the
whole thing is a rhythmic monotone.

And on Eastern art:

I found nothing in the West to compare with Eastern art. Western art has much that is external, sometimes a great deal of philosophy; but Eastern art is precise, mathematical, without
manipulations. It is a form of script.

And on art in general:

Either the shoemaker's craft must be called art, or all contemporary art must be called craft. In what way is a shoemaker sewing
fashionable custom shoes of beautiful design inferior to an artist
who pursues the aim of imitation or originality? *With knowledge,
the sewing of shoes may be sacred art too, but without it, a priest of
contemporary art is worse than a cobbler.*[12]

Any reader who finds the above statements out of character with the
over-all portrait thus far depicted might ponder that remark cited
earlier about the man who 'can sometimes by accident even tell the
truth.'

Gurdjieff, to sum up, made in his way a terrific impresario—only,
on closer examination a superb tinkerer comes nearer the reality,
since the preponderance of his projects and constructions in the
long run seemed ready to—and mostly did—fall apart, on those rare

12. This in its manner recalls Ananda Coomaraswamy's 'The artist is not a special kind of man, but every man a special kind of artist.'

occasions when he did not wilfully tear them down himself, in keeping with what could be called his Law of the Necessity for Incessant Change.

An article appeared in a New York review, *The Century*, a month after the Gurdjieff troupe had made its American tour, by a writer and traveller named G. E. Bechhofer, who first met the thaumaturge at Tiflis and among other things has this to report about a sojourn at Fontainebleau:

> I often heard it said that Gurdjieff was a marvellous worker. The disciples, breathless with rapture, told me of the unusual speed and ease with which he laid out roads, for example, or sawed wood, laid bricks, designed ovens for drying herrings. But recently I have noticed a dubious element in these accounts. The roads did not hold up with wear, the walls cracked, the ovens did not work and dry the herrings. It is possible that Gurdjieff is not the superartisan he was claimed to be.[13]

But what matter if like his material constructions, his elaborate etherial systems, when impartially scrutinized, fall to pieces like a house of cards? The danger only begins when a tinkerer starts tinkering with human souls.

❂

The time has now come to ask what Gurdjieff, or the 'Power', 'Great Source', 'Sarmân Brotherhood', or what not from whom he received his investiture, was really up to. The answer is as simple as it is devastating: *the total upheaval of the world order.* This is not to say that he was up to it, but that he intended it. Total: the combined series of his writings is entitled *All and Everything*, and not just 'this thing and that thing.' The reversal was envisaged, moreover, as coming about in three stages, denoted by the trilogy form which his writings take.

13. This extract was found in Pauwels and has thus had to be re-translated back into English.

To help clarify the pattern, it is revealing to borrow from the language of mystical theology, where the first stage would correspond to the term Purgation. Normally, this means the process undergone by the spiritual aspirant to rid himself of the 'world' with all its illusions and seductions. With Gurdjieff (*First Series*), it means

> to destroy, mercilessly, without any compromise whatsoever, in the mentation and feelings of the reader, the beliefs and views, by centuries rooted in him, about everything existing in the world.

Aimed at here is nothing less than the established dominion of powers formerly and still presently ruling the world—everything political, institutional, social and economic, religious, philosophic, and cultural—at least '*as practiced*' in their existing forms.

Illumination is the second stage in mystical theology, where the adept now emptied of the 'world' is in a spiritual capacity for receiving the Divine influx of graces from the supraformal and Heavenly World. With Gurdjieff (*Second Series*), it means 'to acquaint the reader with the material required for a new creation and to prove the soundness and good quality of it.' What this comes down to in effect is the replacing of the Noumenal World from which our world emanates, in favour of Gurdjieff's phenomenalist cosmology; the replacing of the Celestial Pantheon with its supraformal domains and deities, Divine Qualities and Attributes, Archetypes, Angelic Intelligences, and hierarchy of Powers as revealed by all traditions, in favour of his 'Megalocosmos' with its *Protocosmos*, *Ayocosmos*, *Macrocosmos*, *Deuterocosmos*, *Mesocosmos*, *Tritocosmos*, *Microcosmos*, *Defterocosmos*, plus the bewildering variety of the 'Tetartocosmoses' with their 'temporarily independent crystallizations' named *Protoëhary*, *Defteroëhary*, *Tritoëhary*, *Tetartoëhary*, *Randjoëhary*, *Exioëhary*, and *Resulzarion*—cosmoses peopled and ruled by the likes of the 'Archangel Sakaki', 'Archangel Hariton', 'Arch-cherub Peshtvogner', 'Chief-Common-Universal-Arch-Chemist-Physicist Angel Looisos', 'Most-Great-Arch-Seraph Sevohtartra', 'His Self-Keepness the Archseraph Ksheltarria', 'Very Saintly Ashiata Shiemash', and so forth. Even the sun has to go. Beelzebub is embittered by the malicious results of false education on all three-brained creatures inhabiting the planet earth (with the exception of 'certain beings who existed before the second Transapalnian perturbation') which conditions them into believing down to the last person without the slightest suspicion of doubt that the source of light and heat is the sun, when in reality the 'Sun' is

almost always freezing cold like the 'hairless-dog' of our highly esteemed Mullah Nassr Eddin...[and] perhaps more covered with ice than the surface, of what they call their 'North Pole'.

Indeed, the 'Sun' has better uses for any trace of heat it may possess than to share it with the 'lopsided monstrosity' (ever since the moon was apparently shorn off by a comet) which is our earth.

No, the source of the arisings of light and heat in the cosmos is from the *Iraniranumange* or transformation of energies due to the *Trogoautoegocrat* or Law of Reciprocal Maintenance. The way it works is simplicity itself: within the 'Most Holy Sun Absolute' is the 'Sacred Triarnazikarnno' or principle of 'Holy Affirming', 'Holy-Denying', and 'Holy-Reconciling'[14] which together beget the *Theomertmalogos* or 'Word-God', being the 'prime emanation from which the 'Omnipresent-Okidanokh obtains its prime arising'; for as Bennett explains, 'It is not God that is omnipotent but the Universal Will, the *Okidanokh*.' The 'Vivifyingness of Vibrations' results from the passage of this latter through 'Stopinders' or 'gravity-centers' within the 'fundamental common-cosmic sacred Hepta-paraparshinokh,' which is none other than our Law Seven-foldness. And thus is the cause why the three-brains have 'those cosmic phenomena which they call "daylight", "darkness", "heat", "cold", and so on.'

The final stage in mystical theology is called Realization, or Union. With Gurdjieff (*Third Series*), it means

to assist the arising, in the mentation and in the feelings of the reader, of a veritable, nonfantastic representation not of that illusory world which he now perceives, but of the world existing in reality.

---

14. Here we have an echo of Hegelian thesis, antithesis, and synthesis.

Only this, he says elsewhere, will ease 'the Sorrow of OUR COMMON ENDLESS FATHER.' And there in a nutshell is what Harmonious Development is all about.

❂

Some people tap their heads upon hearing Gurdjieff's theories about the 'moon', but this is to miss the point. The moon for him is not just the physical body in the sky, any more than it is for Dante, who follows mediaeval cosmology in equating the Lunar Sphere with the Terrestrial Paradise and gateway to the Higher Heavens; this accords with the Upanishads, where the waxing moon symbolizes access to Higher States of Being for those on the *deva-yāna* ('Path of the Gods'). But if this phase or face of the moon corresponds to *Janua Coeli*, as in the litanies of the Virgin in the Catholic liturgy, there is also *Janua Inferni* or the waning aspect symbolizing a return to individual states of manifestation for those on the *pitri-yāna* ('Path of the ancestors'). Hence the moon is both Diana and Hecate, door to Heaven and door to Hell, but in either case the Abode of the Dead and *locus* of 'cosmic memory'. 'The Lunar Sphere,' says Guénon, 'determines the separation of the higher (non-individual) states from the lower (individual) states.' For this reason the term *sub-lunary* is a synonym for flux, ephemerality, change, and dissolution.

With Gurdjieff, the moon is

> man's enemy . . . 'at the extremity', at the end of the world; it is the 'outer darkness' of the Christian doctrine 'where there will be weeping and gnashing of teeth.'

While he speaks about the possibility of 'liberation from the moon,' this is really wishful thinking on his part, as his orientation or center of gravity is effectively confined within the subtle domain—whose outermost limit is precisely the Sphere of the Moon—on his own admission that 'everything in the Universe is material.'

'The sun, verily, is life,' says the *Prasna Upanishad*; 'matter, indeed, is the moon.' It is in this cosmological sense that Gurdjieff is a 'materialist', and not in the ordinary usage of the word; that is, everything 'below the moon' pertains to the realm of matter—whether gross or subtle, the subtle state belonging to the individual and not the Universal plane of reality and being comprised of formal manifestation—albeit in a mode 'interiorized' as contrasted with corporeal; psychic or 'animic' rather than physical.

These explanations have a twofold purpose: to show that Gurdjieff's 'worlds' are not simply the luminaries one sees in the skies, and to situate that sector of the cosmos to which his cosmology applies. For neologisms change nothing; his 'worlds' are 'real' enough at their level, even if but a shadowy semblance of the upper hierarchy—worlds merging upon the infraformal rather than the supraformal; and were he to give them their more 'traditional' designations, it would only serve to discomfit when not alienating the reader, and thwart the ends that he—or more accurately his 'Hidden Directorate'—had and has in view. The same goes for the 'Higher Powers' inhabiting these worlds: nothing would be gained for him in using their common appellations. It was already a 'trial balloon'—as his Mullah Nassr Eddin might call it—to put Beelzebub's name on his magnum opus; he certainly would never have entitled it 'Satan's Tales to His Grandson'. But Beelzebub. . . . Well, if not all readers are going to subscribe to the tune on the jacket about this 'all-wise' fellow's 'profound understanding' and 'deep compassion', many will nevertheless find him a harmless enough—if crotchety—old fogy in the long run, who would not even hurt one of those creatures over whom his lordship is firmly established—at least etymologically. Gurdjieff also had in view the idea that familiarity begets derision, for he sought to inure his readers with the injunction to wade thrice through his writings, by which time they should be conditioned for anything—or as he words it:

> Only then can my hope be actualized that according to your understanding you will obtain the specific benefit for yourself which I anticipate, and which I wish for you with all my being.

In addition, he serves a Warning on the readers at the commencement of *Beelzebub* about such mental associations as must engender in them all kinds of automatic contradictory impulses ... owing to the famous what is called 'religious morality' existing and rooted in their life, and in them, consequently, there must inevitably be formed data for an inexplicable hostility towards me personally.

Thus challenged, or flattered as the case may be, certain categories of readers at any rate blithely sail into the book determined to show its author that they, at least, are not victims of 'automatic contradictory impulses,' but on the contrary ready, or 'mature' enough, to master any message he has to offer.[15]

Yet, it might be asked, if this is how things are, why does Gurdjieff not betray hostility towards religion? The obvious answer—apart from the fact that he does, for those who can read between the lines (and according to his disciples, this is the only way to understand his writings)—is, why should he? Of what avail was it for Madame Blavatsky to proclaim: 'Our aim is not to restore Hinduism, but to sweep Christianity off the surface of the earth,' or Annie Besant to unmask her design to 'chase God from Heaven'? Gurdjieff chose rather to manifest toward religion an attitude, in current parlance, of 'benign neglect'. The 'well-foundedness' of this approach is vindicated in the way his followers believe that he and the saints and sages of all traditions are talking about the same thing—the difference for them being simply one of expertise on his part and a more direct access to 'ancient sources'. Let the Great Source by whom he was mandated once gain the ascendancy, and there would then be time enough to deal in whatever style seemed fit with the likes of 'Saints Moses, Jesus, Mohammed, Buddha, Lama [sic],' and the rest, who are anyway already distorted beyond recognition in the portrayals given by the thaumaturge. The preceding section offers examples of the lessons he managed to elicit from Christianity and Islam; and in Beelzebub 'Saint Buddha' himself utters a long

15. The author must have felt his ends in mind were well accomplished, as Beelzebub at the finish of the book is rewarded for his labors with a magnificent new growth of five-pronged horns, reserved solely for those who have attained 'the Reason of the sacred Podkoolad, i.e., the last gradation before the Reason of the sacred Anklad.'

harangue on the organ Kundabuffer which sounds word for word like the credulous Hassein's grandfather speaking.

Still, did Gurdjieff even dream for an instant, however preposterous it seems, that he could inaugurate a movement to replace the Celestial Pantheon or Rule of Heaven with that of the nether spheres, let alone make a dent in society? The answer is, he did the only thing he knew to do, motivated throughout his life by what he calls an 'itching-itch . . . to elucidate everything' by means of 'instilling into the consciousness of my contemporaries of several such "psychic-initiative" factors as in my opinion . . . ought inevitably to act as guiding principles in the consciousness of all creatures presuming to call themselves "God-like"'—fully determined to 'tread heavily on the most sensitive corn of everyone he met' rather than falter by the wayside. We have seen him say, 'I need soldiers who will fight for me for the new world.' Bennett estimates that Gurdjieff must have marshalled some tens of thousands of such soldiers from the time he first started taking pupils around 1909, including upwards of a thousand under his personal supervision at one period or another. Undoubtedly he could even have had many more had he wished; but clearly what he sought was an 'elect', and not just a passing coterie of admirers.

It has already been mentioned how his objectives were confounded by the motor accident at Fontainebleau, regarded by him 'as the manifestation of a power hostile to his aim, a power with which he could not contend.' Bennett speaks of

> the intensity of the forces at work which destroyed, or at least deferred for long years, the hopes that many had formed that Gurdjieff's system might change the course of human history.

But to the end he kept his sights high, and even in the last summer of his life declaimed: 'I am Gurdjieff! I not will die. . . . One day *Beelzebub* will be read in Pope's Palace. Perhaps I will be there.'

Dr Christopher Evans, an experimental psychologist cited in the first part of this expose, writes of the thaumaturge:

> The spell that this extraordinary individual seems to have held over people is really hard to fathom. . . . There seems to have

been an aura or presence about him which it is impossible to comprehend in the language of science and psychology.

This is because Gurdjieff operated out of a domain inaccessible to analytical science, a domain moreover even unsuspected by it to exist. And yet it is this very secret which allows Gurdjieff whatever triumphs he has gained in the modern world. For the true ancients from whom he alleges the origin of his teachings were fully cognizant of this domain and would ironically—if one wishes—by that fact have made the dissemination of any such teachings fall on barren soil—these ancients not having that 'child-like naïveté'—in this sphere, to say the least—which Peters claims was Gurdjieff's design to inculcate in people.

The paradox about Gurdjieff the 'materialist' is the way in which he more than any other figure probably in our day has been able to effectuate a breach in the protective carapace of matter sealing off our world from its animic substratum. If one can judge by Holy Writ, his legacy will not be lost, being but a mild foretaste of what Destiny holds in store; and Gurdjieff even admitted in so many words that he was really a precursor, or 'Herald of Coming Good' as he puts it.

For the reader who desires to see things in a clear light, the whole matter hinges on metaphysical discernment—even if aesthetic discernment alone should suffice.

In order to situate Gurdjieff and his movement, the one and only question the seeker has to resolve is whether or not God is Omnipotent. If the answer is in the affirmative, then Gurdjieff and his hosts are doomed.

Index